Marrakech

Select

contents

Marrakech overview

Marrakech is arguably the most exotic, mysterious and enchanting city this close to Europe. The 'Red City', capital of the Great South, was once a place of such importance that it gave its name to Morocco. Its thousand-year history is rich and turbulent, with an eclectic cast of characters: sultans and princesses, magicians and slave-traders, fortune-hunters and colonialists. Now it attracts movie stars, writers and artists – and tourists looking for something a bit different.

In the 1960s and '70s, Marrakech lured hippies, playboys, rich expats and the fashion elite. It was one of the coolest and also the most artistically inspiring places to escape to and, often, reinvent yourself in. Today, Marrakech is experiencing its latest renaissance. With colourful souks and spectacular riads in the ancient medina; a fabulous array of restaurants, bars, cafés and art galleries in Guéliz (the new town or Ville Nouvelle); blissfully tranquil villa retreats; some of the best

boutique and five-star hotels in the world, and a wealth of adventures to be had on its doorstep – from skiing to hot-air ballooning and camel-trekking to horse-riding – this desert city at the crossroads of cultures has reinvented itself yet again as a hip, romantic, adventurous getaway for those who want a little spice in their holiday.

Marrakech is undoubtedly not for everyone. This is a city with edge. It is contradictory and not easily fathomed, but for most people who visit, that is all part of its elusive charm. From the exotic market stalls of the medina to the westernised glamour of the Ville Nouvelle, Marrakech is a riot of contradictions and extremes – at once African and Arab, eastern and western, frontier town and modern city, religious and secular, elegant and rough-round-the-edges. At times daunting, occasionally maddening, always exhilarating, Marrakech is all about getting lost, letting go and opening up to whatever experience or encounter comes your way.

in the mood for...

...souks, boutiques and markets

From the souks filled with exotic treasures and stalls of spices piled high to fabulously chic boutiques selling everything from kaftans to kids' clothes, you could be forgiven for thinking that Marrakech is all about the shopping. For many it is, and exploring the magical labyrinthine **souks** *(p.38)* should be first on your list of things to do in the city. Watch master craftsmen at work and haggle for lanterns, carpets, soft leather slippers *(babouches)* and Berber jewellery.

For foodies, the colourful **Mellah Market** *(p.65)* in the old Jewish quarter is an essential stop, where you will find seasonal fruit and veg, flowers, preserved lemons and olives, roses and butchers' stalls. There is also **Spice Square** *(p.40)*, lined with apothecaries brimming with thousands of different spices, plus lotions and potions, cosmetics and even chameleons for sale. If you're in the market for a carpet, the **Criée Berbère** *(p.50)* is the place to go and if it's serious gold jewellery, head to the dazzling **Grande Bijouterie** *(p.76)*.

Vintage lovers won't be disappointed either. Not only are the main souks dotted with antique stores selling everything from Leicas to 1950s Coca Cola signs, but the northern medina has one of the best flea markets south of Paris. **Souk el Khemis** (*p.93*) is a little-known goldmine where you will find Victorian gramophones, 19th-century oil paintings, 1960s furniture and painted doors from 500 year-old riads. Fittingly for a city like Marrakech, there are some real-life **Aladdin's caves** (*p.92*) in the medina, where movie producers and celebrities are known to shop.

If you are craving a western hit where things come with price tags, there are dozens of new **boutiques in the medina** (La Galerie, *p.45* and Rue Riad Zitoun el Jdid, *p.73*), several high-end antique places on **Rue Dar el Bacha** (*p.91*) and a wealth of shops in **Guéliz** (*p.103*), where you can find Western takes on kaftans, stylish homewares and even Moroccan haute couture.

... street food

Western restaurants with price tags to match are springing up all over Marrakech and it's sometimes easy to forget that you are in Morocco, not Paris or London. There is no more vivid reminder of where you are, and no more authentic or unusual eating experience to be had, than through Marrakech's street food. Underrated and often wrongly viewed with apprehension, street food is an exotic taste-fest and a window onto a different world.

The soul of Marrakech street food is found at the **food stalls of Jemaa el Fna** *(p.32)*, where you can eat anything from snails to grilled sheep's head and from spicy merguez sausages to succulent chicken brochettes for just a few dirhams. There are stalls and makeshift restaurants all over the city, for this is how most Moroccans eat when they are not at home, but **Méchoui Alley** *(p.53)* and long-standing institution, **Chez Bejgueni**, in Guéliz *(p.121)* should not be missed.

... a spectacle

The whole city of Marrakech is a spectacle and just walking through the medina can throw up a lively hotchpotch of experiences and encounters. But the beating heart of the city's theatrical soul is the square of **Jemaa el Fna** *(p.32)*, where a thrilling thousand year-old nightly show (some call it the greatest on earth) unfolds like a magic carpet at sunset. There are acrobats and magicians, storytellers and snake charmers and all manner of spontaneous entertainment in between. And, contrary to popular assumption, this is not just a display for tourists, who are far outnumbered by animated locals.

By day, it is the preserve of Gnaoua musicians, apothecaries, dentists, witch doctors, orange juice sellers and dancing monkeys. This is also the place to visit a **fortune-teller** *(p.37)* – an ancient practice still thriving in a country where concepts of superstition and *baraka* (luck) are threaded through society.

... pampering

Souks, spectacles, adventures and fine dining aside, you could come to Marrakech just for the spas. The art of the hammam (or steam bath) is ancient, dating back millennia, and is an essential part of both religious and social life in the Arab world. Cleanliness is one of the basic tenets of Islam, water is considered sacred and the hammam is as much a part of daily life in Morocco as the mosque. This is where people come to socialise with friends, catch up on neighbourhood gossip, discuss business and even arrange marriages.

In Marrakech, virtually every hotel these days has a spa or hammam, so for many you won't even need to leave your hotel to get pampered. Visiting a traditional, local hammam, such as the **Hammam Dar el Bacha** *(p.99)*, where you will be flung into the heart of communal life and scrubbed to within an inch of your life, may not be everyone's idea of heaven but it's an authentic Moroccan experience

and will illuminate a corner of Marrakchi life usually hidden from tourists.

For those who want a more refined spa, without losing the other-worldly charm of a traditional hammam, there is **Les Bains de Marrakech** *(p.64)*, where oriental perfectly combines with modern. For urbanites, there are the super-slick spas of Guéliz: **Les Secrets de Marrakech** *(p.113)*, **Es Saadi** *(pictured; p.113)* and the **Bab Hotel** *(p.110);* here, facials, manicures and massages are carried out in beautifully designed modern rooms and you

have the added bonus of being round the corner from some of the best shops and restaurants in Marrakech.

But for the very pinnacle of pampering, the loftiest heights of uber-luxe indulgence are to be found in the exclusive spas of five-star hotels, such as the **Royal Mansour** *(p.52)*, the **Ksar Char-Bagh** and the **Four Seasons** *(both on p.170)*, where the best in modern cosmetics and spa treatments are combined with almost unimaginably decadent and romantic surroundings.

... Arabian Nights

A candlelit table strewn with roses in the courtyard of a 500 year-old house, the starry African night above, course after course of exotically flavoured dishes... Dinner in a riad in Marrakech is as close as you'll get to a real-life Arabian Nights experience.

For pure romance, there is **Dar Yacout**, where movie stars and royalty like to eat, and **Dar Zellij** *(both on p.90)*, set in a glamorous original 17th century courtyard and with a sumptuous menu.

For the best French food in town, eaten in a whitewashed courtyard hung with vintage carpets and tables set under fragrant orange trees, it can only be **Le Pavillon** *(p.90)*. **Le Fondouk** *(p.96)* is located in a beautifully restored old artisanal riad, where Marrakech's vibrant history as a trading city permeates the atmosphere. For post-dinner Moroccan glamour, there is belly dancing at **Le Comptoir** and live music at the opulent **Jad Mahal** *(both on p.126)*.

... decadent days

As Mae West once said, 'too much of a good thing can be wonderful!' Plunge pools on rooftops, luxurious villas in exotic gardens, exquisite cooking... For lazily decadent days, Marrakech has it all.

Several glorious riad hotels in the medina are open to non-residents. Give yourself some down time at **Les Jardins de la Koutoubia**, **Riad el Fenn** or **Les Jardins de la Medina** *(all p.46)*, all of which have stunning pools, delicious food and sumptuous spas.

The five star resorts of **Sofitel** and **Es Saadi** *(p.130)* are good options for indulging yourself in Hivernage. If visiting just for lunch isn't enough, stay at a riad where you can indulge in aquatic bliss as often as you like: **La Sultana**, **Les Borjs de la Kasbah** *(pictured)* and **Riad Kaiss** *(p.67)* are three of the best.

For the ultimate decadent treat, have tea or cocktails at **La Mamounia** *(p.70)* or spend the whole day at a **poolside oasis** outside town *(p.128)*.

13

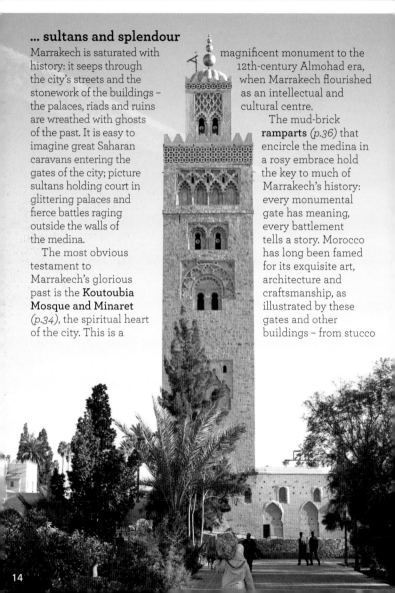

... sultans and splendour

Marrakech is saturated with history: it seeps through the city's streets and the stonework of the buildings – the palaces, riads and ruins are wreathed with ghosts of the past. It is easy to imagine great Saharan caravans entering the gates of the city; picture sultans holding court in glittering palaces and fierce battles raging outside the walls of the medina.

The most obvious testament to Marrakech's glorious past is the **Koutoubia Mosque and Minaret** *(p.34)*, the spiritual heart of the city. This is a magnificent monument to the 12th-century Almohad era, when Marrakech flourished as an intellectual and cultural centre.

The mud-brick **ramparts** *(p.36)* that encircle the medina in a rosy embrace hold the key to much of Marrakech's history: every monumental gate has meaning, every battlement tells a story. Morocco has long been famed for its exquisite art, architecture and craftsmanship, as illustrated by these gates and other buildings – from stucco

carved like lace and finely painted cedar wood doorways to jewel-like *zellige* tilework and delicately soaring arches and columns.

This is a country that has always celebrated beauty and splendour. Nowhere is this better illustrated than in the atmospheric ruins of the 16th-century **Badi Palace** *(p.74)*, which were once adorned with marble and gold, and in the spectacular courtyards of the **Bahia Palace** *(pictured; p.62)*, where sultans held sway.

The glittering **Saadian Tombs** *(p.66)* are a fitting resting place for the kings of Morocco. To find out more about the past, head for the **Musée de Marrakech** *(p.86)*, where you can learn about the city's history amid a splendid collection of Moroccan arts and crafts.

The **Madrassa Ben Youssef** *(p.82)* is one of the most tranquil and architecturally inspiring buildings in the city, while the remarkable **Koubba** *(p.101)*, the oldest building in Marrakech, evokes bygone worlds. Finally, the **Chroub ou Chouf** fountain *(p.100)*, dating from the 16th century (and in need of repair), is a fitting example of the importance of water here on the edge of the desert.

... a glamorous night out

Nights in Marrakech can sparkle with glitz and glamour if that is what you're after. You can have cocktails looking out over the city's tiled rooftops at the **Bab Hotel** and **Renaissance Bar** *(p.110)* or you can listen to funky live music at **Kechmara**, **African Chic** *(both p.116)* and **Jad Mahal** *(p.126)*.

The hip crowd hangs out at **Bo et Zin** and **Le Comptoir** *(pictured)* and die-hard clubbers head to **Pacha**, **Theatro** and **Silver** *(all on p.126)*. If you want to try your hand at the gaming table, there are two casinos *(p.132)*.

... a literary afternoon

From Ibn Battuta's *Travels* to Esther Freud's *Hideous Kinky*, Marrakech has inspired a thousand stories and been muse to dozens of writers.

A favourite haunt of the Spanish writer Juan Goytisolo is the **Café de France** *(p.47)* in the Jemaa el Fna, which is also where Peter Mayne wrote *A Year in Marrakesh*. **Dar Cherifa** *(pictured; p.43)* is a gorgeous temple to literature and art in the heart of the medina, while in Guéliz you'll find **Café du Livre** *(p.117)*, where hours can be whiled away in the peaceful library-cum-bookshop-cum-restaurant.

... a bit of peace and quiet

Marrakech can be hectic, hot and dusty, but it also has peaceful sanctuaries where you can get away from it all. The Red City has been famous for hundreds of years for its luxuriant gardens. Yves Saint Laurent's **Jardin Majorelle** *(pictured; p.106)* is one of the most iconic in the world and a magical spot to spend an afternoon. The **Agdal Gardens** *(p.68)* were created for the sultan's pleasure and today are the perfect place for picnics. There is nowhere more atmospheric than the **Menara Gardens and Pavilion** *(p.127)* at sunset, with its backdrop of snow-capped Atlas Mountains. But even in the thick of things and in the most unlikely places are hidden refuges. In the medina, there are **rooftop restaurants** far above the madding crowds, and the **Jewish cemetery** *(p.69)* and **European cemetery** *(p.112)* are unusual yet quietly beautiful places of reflection.

... sporting adventure

If your idea of a holiday is to be as active as possible, Marrakech is surprisingly well equipped, with places where you can keep fit and engage in a variety of sports. Not only are many of the facilities first-class, but enthusiasts can enjoy one of the best climates in the world, with almost year-round sunshine, very little rain and warm temperatures that only become uncomfortably hot in the months of July and August.

Although golf is controversial, due to its excessive use of water, Marrakech is positioning itself as one of the world's premier golfing destinations (the king is a keen golfer). Many of the courses (*p.134*) are exotically

landscaped and dramatically situated, with amazing views of the High Atlas. Fit for a king and Winston Churchill, the **Royal Golf de Marrakech** is the oldest course in Morocco and still one of the best. Designed by Robert Trent Jones, the **Palmeraie Golf Palace** is a firm favourite and the **Amelkis Golf Resort** and **Samanah Country Club** both offer challenging golf on stunning courses.

If it's tennis you prefer, the **Royal Tennis Club**, **Es Saadi** and the multi-activity **Palmeraie Golf Palace** *(p.130)* all offer good clay tennis courts in beautifully-kept grounds. At the tranquil retreat of **La Pause** *(p.150)* you can

ride a horse in the Agafay Desert, as well as play mini golf or go **quad-biking**, with miles of exhilarating trails to explore and several good companies offering quad-biking day trips *(p.152)*. For a more romantic (and eco-friendly) adventure, you can experience the thrill of a **hot-air balloon ride** over the city *(p.137)*.

Some may find that **skiing** on the highest pistes in North Africa *(p.145)*, just an hour from Marrakech, or **bicycling** through the alleys of the medina *(p.85)* are the ultimate quirky experiences, while others think a mini **camel safari** *(p.136)* through ancient palm groves is the quintessential Moroccan adventure.

... a gourmet experience

Marrakech is a food-lover's paradise, a haven for afficionados of exotic tastes, with influences from Africa, the Middle East and France all combining to make an exciting cuisine – the food is definitely one of the highlights of a visit here.

Discover the perfect ingredients in the bustling **Mellah Market** (*p.65*) and the charismatic, pungent **Spice Square** (*p.40*). Enjoy a Marrakchi speciality of **slow roast lamb** at Méchoui Alley (*p.53*). Learn how to cook a traditional tagine or pastilla at the cookery school of **La Maison Arabe** (*p.88*). For a Moroccan feast fit for a sultan, splurge at **Le Tobsil** or **Dar Moha** (*p.48*). If it all gets too much, refresh your palate at one of the best **Asian restaurants** in town, **Katsura,** (*p.118*) or in the nostalgically colonial surroundings of **La Bagatelle** (*p.109*) or **Grand Café de la Poste** (*p.111*). If you have a sweet tooth, seek out some delicious **pâtisserie** (*p.120*).

... fine art

Artists have been drawn to Morocco for centuries, but in the 21st century it is home-grown Moroccan artists that are capturing the imagination. If you think Marrakech is all about the past, think again.

In the medina, there is the fabulous **Ministero del Gusto** *(pictured; p.41)*, a world of pure fantasy at the pinnacle of quirky creativity. The **Dar Si Said Museum** *(p.72)* has one of the best exhibitions of Moroccan arts and crafts in the world, while **Maison Tiskiwin** *(p.77)* takes you on myriad journeys through the collection of a veteran anthropologist and explorer. The beautiful photographs at **Maison de la Photographie** *(p.87)* reveal a Morocco that once was, while at the cutting edge of the contemporary Moroccan art scene are dozens of fantastically stimulating contemporary **art galleries** *(p.114)* in Guéliz, which should be at the top of all art lovers' lists.

... escaping the city

Taking a day trip outside Marrakech illuminates a completely different Morocco and opens windows onto worlds that can surpass your wildest imaginings. Whether you choose to explore mountain, rural or coastal Morocco – all of which are within surprisingly easy reach of Marrakech – you will encounter famously hospitable people, revel in some of the most glorious landscapes on earth and have an experience that you will remember forever.

The **High Atlas Mountains** *(p.142)* are just an hour from Marrakech, and the region around Mount Toubkal and the village of Imlil offers a wealth of hiking and trekking possibilities in a magnificent part of Morocco that has changed little in centuries. The gently rolling foothills of the Atlas are also studded with charming places to spend the day and restaurants with breathtaking views, such as **La Bergerie**, **La Roseraie** and **L'Oliveraie** *(p.144)*.

For a true breath of fresh air, the **Ourika Valley** *(p.146)* is a

rural utopia, with eco-museums, hotels and aromatic gardens to discover.

If you feel the need for cool refreshing water after the dust of the city, head for the seven waterfalls of **Setti Fatma** *(p.148)* or the dramatic **Cascades d'Ouzoud** *(p.153)*.

Adrenalin junkies are spoilt for choice, with **helicopter rides** *(p.151)* over the Atlas and into the Sahara for lunch, **skiing** *(p.145)* in the retro French-style resort of Oukaimeden and **quad-biking** *(p.152)* through palm groves and desert terrain. There is horse-

riding and days of silence to be had just 45 minutes from Marrakech in the **Agafay Desert** *(p.150)*, and **Lalla-Takerkoust** *(p.149)*, a stunning lake at the foot of the High Atlas, is ringed with excellent restaurants.

For the ultimate day trip, have lunch by the sea in enchanting **Essaouira** *(p.154)*. This windswept town has everything: characterful white-washed buildings, fresh seafood, a vast crescent of golden beach where the windsurfing, surfing and kite-surfing is first-class, and a sleepy medina full of antique shops and art galleries.

neighbourhoods

Marrakech is divided into the medina (the old town) and Guéliz (the Ville Nouvelle or new town). To help you get around, we've divided the medina into central, northern and southern neighbourhoods. Guéliz is a separate neighbourhood; Hivernage, the Menara, Palmeraie and environs are covered in a separate chapter, and excursions in the Marrakech region are highlighted in the final section.

Central Medina This is the geographical heart, spiritual soul and tourist hub of the medina. Everything in this area – demarcated at its southern end by the gardens of the Koutoubia and at its northern edge by Rue Dar el Bacha – revolves like a whirlpool around the iconic Jemaa el Fna with its ancient nightly spectacle. The souks stretch north of the square, and the magnificent Koutoubia Mosque at the neighbourhood's western edge stands sentinel over the whole of Marrakech.

Southern Medina The grandest part of the medina, this southern neighbourhood has a colourful cultural history and is where you'll find many of the city's most chic riads. Made up predominantly of the original fortified kasbah, the royal palace and the Mellah (Jewish quarter) with its colourful markets, the area is punctuated by the great imperial palaces of Marrakech, some wonderful museums celebrating the city's heritage, the legendary Mamounia hotel and the Agdal Gardens, where Marrakchis picnic in summer.

Northern Medina Far from the mania of the souks, the northern triangle of the medina is, for the most part, refreshingly undiscovered. Traditional, tranquil residential life is played out around the tomb of Marrakech's most revered patron saint, Sidi Bel Abbes; vintage-lovers can spend hours exploring the chaotic rambling flea market of Souk el Khemis; south, closer to the souks, are galleries, fondouks, boutique shops, romantic riad restaurants, a scattering of tailor's shops and hammams, and the atmospheric Madrassa Ben Youssef.

Guéliz Often undeservedly overlooked, super-relaxed Guéliz (the new town or Ville Nouvelle as it is known) has some of the best and most varied restaurants in town – from sushi and Thai to Lebanese, Italian and French. Its leafy side streets are dotted with charming shops where everything has a price tag and there is no need to haggle; fantastic modern art galleries showcasing Moroccan and international artists; outdoor cafés that are great for people-watching, and Yves Saint Laurent's Jardin Majorelle, a breathtaking sanctuary in the heart of the city.

Hivernage, Menara, Palmeraie, Environs Hivernage, the wealthy residential district, is all about private houses and large chain hotels, but it also has some of the best nightclubs and hippest bars in town. On the edge of Marrakech is the mesmerizing Menara pavilion and to the north is the fabled Palmeraie, home to some of the most luxurious villas, spas and exclusive hotels in Morocco. Nearby, there are tennis and golf clubs, while the more adventurous can head off on a camel safari or take a hot-air balloon ride.

Marrakech Region Within two hours of Marrakech an extraordinary range of adventures can be had. From lunching beside the serene waters of Lake Lalla-Takerkoust to surfing the crashing breakers of Essaouira on the Atlantic coast; from skiing in the morning to horse riding in a fiery desert in the afternoon and from the high-adrenalin thrill of a helicopter ride to the horizontally-relaxed vibe of a country restaurant with a panoramic view, the region of Marrakech exemplifies the diversity of Morocco in dazzling microcosm.

25

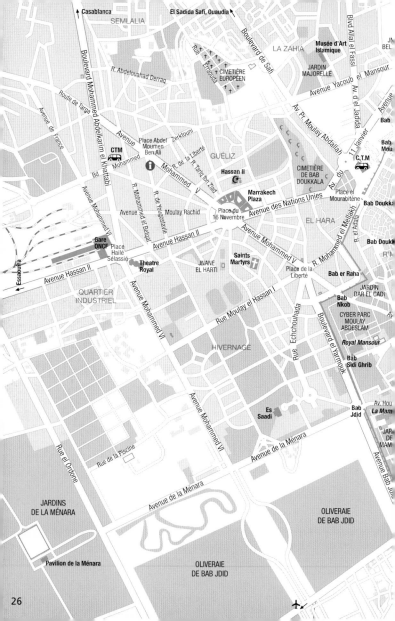

Marrakech

0   250   500 m

0   250   500 yds

N

Palmeraie

KAÂ EL MECHRÂ

Souk el Khemis

CIMETIÈRE DE TAGOURIANTE

Oued Issil

Route des Ramparts

ANE ABBÈS

Bab el Jnane Bel Abbès

el Arset Brahim

Kaâ el Mechrâa

CIMETIÈRE SIDI AHMED EZ ZAQUIA

Rue de Bab el Khemis

Bab el Khemis

Bab Kechich

UR JDAD

Zaouia Sidi Bel Abbès

CIMETIÈRE SIDI BEL ABBÈS

SIDI GHALEM

DOUAR TABHIRT

Rue Assouel

Rue de Bab Taghtout

Mosque of Sidi Slimane

Bab el Fakharine

CIMETIÈRE SIDI ECH CHEFFAJ

CIMETIÈRE SIDI MAATI BEN SALAH

Rue el Gza

ASSOUEL

EL MOUKEF

Bab Dbagh

Route des Ramparts

SIDI ALI BENNAÇER

MEDINA

Médersa Ben Youssef

Tanneries

ukkala

Ben Youssef

Rue Bab Debbagh

Koubba el Baroudiyn

R. Dar el Bacha

Musée de Marrakech

Bab Lalla Aouda

Dar el Bacha

Souk Haddadine

ESSEBTIYNE

Souk des Smata

Souk des Sebbaghine

Rue Azbest

Bab Aylen

Cadi Ayad

Mouassine

Kissarias

Souk el Kebir

Dar Cherifa

Rahba Kedima

Sidi Ben Salah

Route des Ramparts

R. Sidi el Yamani

Quessabine

Souks

Place Sidi Youb

R. el Cadi Ayad

R. Sidi el Yamani

Rue Mouassine

Rue Dabachi

ARSET EL MESFIOUI

R. el Cadi Ayad

Sidi Moulay el Ksour

Kharbouch

ARSET EL HOUTA

Bab el Ksour

Jemaa el Fna

KENNARIA

Rue Douar Graoua

JNANE BOUSSEKRI

Rue Bab Ahmad

Place de Foucauld

Palais Moulay Idriss

oubia

JARDINS DE LA OUTOUBIA ouki

Rue Riad Zitoun el Jdid

Dar Si Said

AGUEDAL BAB AHMAD

Bab Ghmat

Place Youssef Ben Tachfine

Avenue Houmman el Fetouaki

Rue Riad Zitoun el Kdim

Palais el Bahia

Sidi Youssef Ben Ali

R. Sidi Mimoun

Maison Tiskiwin

Grande Bijouterie

CIMETIÈRE JUIF DE MIÂARA

CIMETIÈRE BAB GHEMAT

Palais med VI

ARSET EL MAACH

Rue Arset el Maâch

MELLAH

Lazama

Rue Belaïd

Mellah Market

Place des Ferblantiers

BERRIMA

JNANE EL AFIA

Palais er Rob

Kasbah

Palais el Badi

R de Berrima

Bab Agnaou

Tombeaux Saadiens (Saadian Tombs)

KASBAH

Berrima

Bab Jnane el Afia

ERE JNANE ES ILI

Bab er Rob

Palais Royal

Bab el Harri

ARSET BAB ER RÔB

Bab Ahmar

Bab er Ryal

R. de Bab Ahmar

Bab La'yal

Avenue Bab Jdid

Bab Kasbah

Bab Irhli

Bab el Aghdar

Bab er Rih

Avenue Roulis

i, Taroudant

R. de Bab Irhli

Oukaïmeden, Ourika

JARDINS DE L'AGDAL

Ouarzazate

Central Medina

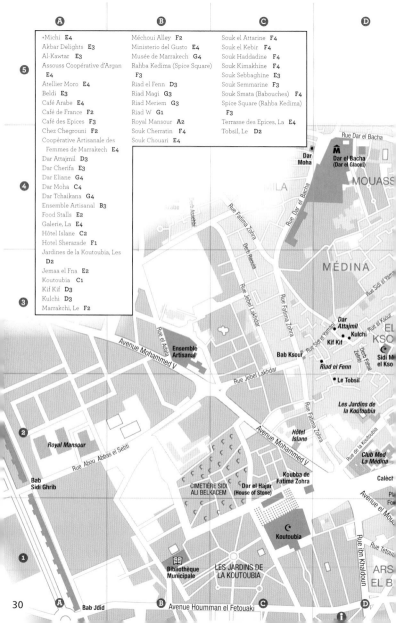

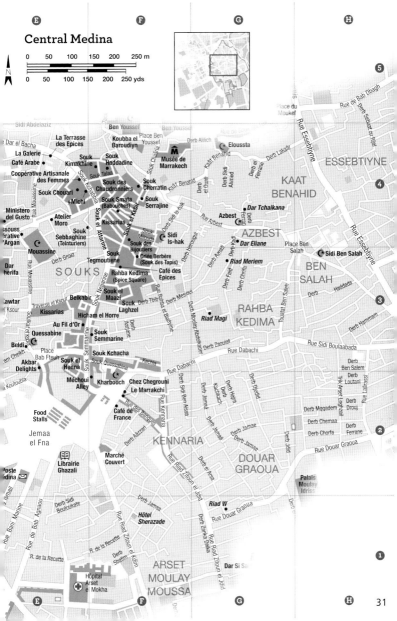

E   **F**   **G**   **H**

0   50   100   150   200   250 m

0   50   100   150   200   250 yds

N

5

Place du Moukef

Rue de Bab Dbagh

Rue Essebtiyne

Rue de Bab Sebaat ou Riat

Sidi Abdelaziz

Ben Youssef   Ben Youssef

Koubba el   Place Ben   Derb Allich

Dar el Bacha   Baroudiyn   Youssef

La Terrasse   Eloussta

des Epices

Kaat Benahid

ESSEBTIYNE

La Galerie

Café Arabe   Souk   Musée de Marrakech

Coopérative Artisanale   Kimakhine   Souk

des Femmes   Souk Talaa   Haddadine

KAAT BENAHID

Derb el Ferrane

Derb Sidi Ahmad

Souk Chouari   Souk des   Souk

Chaudronniers   Cherratin

Michi   Souk Smata   Souk

Atelier   (Babouches)   Serrajine

Ministerio   Moro

del Gusto

Azbest   Dar Tchaikana

Souk   Kissarias

Sebbaghine   Souk des

(Teinturiers)   Bijoutiers

AZBEST

Dar el Quanti

ssouss erative   Argan

Sidi

Is-hak

Dar Eliane

Place Ben Salah

Sidi Ben Salah

Mouassine   Souk

Tegmoutiene   Criée Berbère

(Souk des Tapis)

Riad Meriem

BEN SALAH

Derb Haddada

Dar herifa   **SOUKS**   Rahba Kedima   Café des

(Spice Square)   Epices

Souk el

Maazi   Belkabir   Souk

Riad Magi

RAHBA KEDIMA

Derb Hammam

3

awtar   Kissarias

Ksour   Hicham el Horre   Laghzel

Au Fil d'Or   Souk

Semmarine

Rue Sidi Boulaabada

Quessabine

Beldi   Souk Kchacha

Place

Bab Fteuh

Akbar   Souk el

Delights   Henna   Souk Quessabine

Kechla

Rue Dabachi

Derb Ben Salem

Derb Loutani

Derb Trik Arset Loghlali

Derb Drouj

Méchoui   Kharbouch   Chez Chegrouni

Alley

Le Marrakchi

Food

Stalls   Café de

France

Derb Mqqadem   Derb Chemaa   Derb Chorfa

Derb Ferrane

2

Jemaa

el Fna

KENNARIA

Rue Douar Graoua

Librairie

Ghazali   Marché

Couvert

DOUAR GRAOUA

Poste edina

Hôtel

Sherazade   Riad W   Rue Douar Graoua

Palais Moulay Idriss

1

Hôpital

Arset

el Mokha

ARSET MOULAY MOUSSA

Dar Si Sa

Watch one of the **greatest shows on earth** unfold in the main square of **Jemaa el Fna**

Jemaa el Fna, the iconic physical and cultural heart of Marrakech, is a primal, ancient, intangible space that has been referred to as, 'an inland, tideless sea'. Gathering place for a thousand years, this is where the great Saharan caravans, laden with spices, slaves and salt would arrive from Timbuktu. Today, the goods may have changed, but not the sense that here Africa and Arabia converge. At once circus, open-air food festival and living museum, it is the distillation of Marrakech's mystique and magic.

At first glance, Jemaa el Fna is uninspiring. But spend a few hours here and the essence of this place will slowly reveal itself. During the day, it is the preserve of orange-juice vendors, nut and dried fruit stalls (fill paper bags for munching on), water-sellers, Berber women who will tattoo your hands and feet in henna,

dentists with displays of human teeth, herbalists selling powdered bones and ostrich eggs, Gnaoua musicians with their noisy castanet-like *qraqabs*, chained monkeys and small boys hawking tissues or toys made in China.

But when the muezzin calls and the sun sinks, everything changes. Now, Jemaa el Fna's famous **food stalls** materialize and the fragrant smoke from a hundred *grillades* wafts into the night air. Beneath the glow of a single bulb, families laugh and eat, while around them the music of the Gnaoua mingles with the dying cries of the muezzin, the shouts of competing food vendors and the excited buzz of hundreds of people soaking up the atmosphere.

In the shadows are dozens of ever-expanding and decreasing circles of men. These are the famed *halqias* (storytellers) whose job is to entertain and enthrall. You may see a magician vanishing something into thin air, a snake-charmer playing his haunting flute or – if you are lucky – a wizened man in a cloak telling a tale in classical Arabic with an egg and a length of rope as illustrative props. These storytellers are a dying breed, but they remain the soul of Jemaa el Fna and the reason why the space was declared one of Unesco's first Masterpieces of the Oral and Intangible Heritage of Humanity. It is the people that make Jemaa el Fna what it is, filling the space with its unique energy.

Experiencing Jemaa el Fna is all about diving into the madness. But if it gets a bit much, take sanctuary in one of the restaurants that line the square. For lunch, **Chez Chegrouni** is an old favourite with a fantastic roof terrace and excellent, simple Moroccan food with vegetarian options. Get there early to bag a table with a view. **Le Marrakchi** is a rather beautiful tourist trap with expensive food and belly-dancers but it is the only place on the square that serves alcohol so is tempting for a cocktail at sunset.

Chez Chegrouni; Jemaa el Fna; tel: 0665 47 46 15; B, L, D; map F2
Le Marrakchi; Jemaa el Fna; tel: 0524 44 33 77; B, L, D ; map F2

Soak up the **atmosphere at sunset** when the muezzin calls from **Koutoubia's minaret**

When the sun sets, the haunting sound of the *muezzin* calling out the evening prayer fills the twilight air. The *isha'a* – the last of the five daily prayers, (one of the Pillars of Islam) – is particularly magical.

In Marrakech, the **Koutoubia Mosque** (Mosque of the Booksellers – so named because it was once surrounded by booksellers; map C1) is the first to lead the call – with hundreds of others following in an echo that washes across the city. Unusually, all the calls to prayer here are 'live'; in most other Islamic countries they are recorded. Built in the 12th century by the Almohad caliph, Yacoub el Mansour, the minaret is the tallest structure in Marrakech at nearly 70m (230ft) and exactly five times as high as it is wide. A masterpiece of design, it was the model for the Tour Hassan in Rabat and the Giralda in Seville. Although the mosque is closed to non-Muslims, the *minbar*, from which the imam would lead the prayers, can be seen in the Badi Palace (*p.74*).

The best place to soak up this atmosphere is from the tranquil **Koutoubia gardens**, which afford a wonderful close-up view of the minaret glowing against the indigo sky, or from the roof of the **Hotel Islane** opposite.

Hotel Islane; 279 Avenue Mohammed V; tel: 0524 440 081; www.islane-hotel. com; map C2

FOUR GLOBES

Traditionally, every minaret is surmounted by three globes at the very top of the tower, but the Koutoubia has four. Legend has it that these globes were once made of gold and that the fourth globe was forged out of the melted-down jewellery of Yacoub el Mansour's wife as her penance for breaking one day of the Ramadan fast.

Test your tastebuds and try something new at Marrakech's legendary food stalls

Marrakech's **food stalls**, on Jemaa el Fna (map E2), are arguably the most famous in the world. For this reason, they may seem like just another tourist trap but this is one of the few places where an average Marrakchi family will eat out.

Eating here is an experience not to be missed and one that you will never forget. For those who are prepared to sample the unusual and quirky delights of the stalls, there is an art to this open-air extravaganza. Word of mouth is key. If someone in-the-know has recommended a particular stall, eat there. Failing that, go to the ones that are full of locals. An empty stall on a busy night is not a good sign. Don't be put off by vendors waving menus in your face and herding you towards their stall as they wax lyrical in a dozen languages. Retain your sense of humour. Don't be afraid to try something new. **Mustafa No. 1**'s snails are famously good and the grilled **sheep's head** is surprisingly tasty. For the less adventurous, **merguez sausages**, **kefta** (spicy meatballs), hearty **harira** soup (lentil, chick pea and tomato) and succulent **chicken brochettes** are classic Moroccan street food favourites.

Some stalls also have deliciously simple **grilled fish**, served with a wedge of lemon, a pile of chips and spicy green chili on the side. Sit wherever there is space, shout your order at the chef and tuck in. Eating is done with your hands (always use your right), drinks are soft and the whole thing – along with the crazy theatrical spectacular that is Jemaa el Fna – will set you back just a few dirhams. Foodie heaven.

Ride around the **medina walls** in a **horse-drawn carriage**

Marrakech's calèches – horse-drawn carriages – are as much a part of the city as the mosques and motorbikes. For something a little bit different and a lot more atmospheric, take a ride in the evening when the walls are dramatically lit by the setting sun.

The main calèche stand is on Place du Foucauld (map D2) next to Jemaa el Fna. The **Tour des Ramparts** takes in all 16km of Marrakech's medina walls. The oldest parts date to the foundation of Marrakech in the 12th century and were built by Almoravid sultan Ali Ben Youssef to protect the city from Almohad attack. The walls – 10 metres high, 2 metres thick and built out of pisé (rammed earth) – are punctuated by 18 gates, or *babs*. **Bab el Khemis** (Thursday Gate) marks the entrance to Marrakech's fantastic flea market (*p.93*), **Bab Dbagh** (Gate of the Tanners) leads to the pungent tanneries, **Bab Ghmat**, was breached by Almohad mercenaries in 1147 as they laid siege to the city; **Bab Agnaou** (Black Gate) – a soaring horseshoe arch with intricate carvings framed by inscriptions of the Qur'an – is the most magnificent of them all and the entrance to the royal kasbah, and **Bab Ahmar** (Red Gate) was built by the Almohads exclusively to be used by sultans to gain entry to their palaces.

The carriages fit four people and you should agree the price before you set off. It should be no more than 100dh for an hour.

Have your **hands painted with henna** or your **fortune told** on the Jemaa el Fna

Most people flock to Jemaa el Fna in the evening, when the square is at its most dramatic. But by day, particularly in the late afternoon, Jemaa el Fna can be just as fascinating, with all manner of goings on – from dentists to herbalists, acrobats and water sellers. Perhaps one of the most exotic things you can do at this time of day is have your fortune told. Seek out a fortune teller before the rush of evening descends and absorb a pre-Islamic practice that is still deeply rooted in Moroccan life. The art of henna painting is another ancient tradition that survives in Morocco, and Jemaa el Fna is dotted with women who will paint your hands and feet in a range of designs. The use of henna is still an intrinsic part of any celebration, especially female rites of passage such as the night before a wedding when the bride is adorned. The pattern and symbols of a henna design are as much about beauty as about imparting protection and *baraka* (luck), and the placement of a design also has meaning. For those who want more peaceful surroundings to the Jemaa el Fna, **Peacock Pavilions** *(p.133)* has retreats that include henna painting afternoons.

Get lost in a world of **kaleidoscopic colour** in **souk shopping heaven**

The souks of Marrakech are the largest in Morocco and famed throughout the world as one of the most exotic places in the world to shop. They are also the oldest part of a city that thrived on commerce – and still does.

Historically, all souks were divided and laid out according to separate commodities being made and sold, with the most valuable products (gold, manuscripts) positioned in the centre of the main souk area and lesser goods radiating out from there. Today, little has changed. Each souk is still named after the product being sold and, aside from allowances for modern tastes, the goods are much as they would have been a thousand years ago.

The souks thread north from Jemaa el Fna and continue in a winding labyrinth until they hit the **Musée de Marrakech** (p.86). Open from around 9am to 9pm, the best time to visit is in the cool of morning, or in the evening when the sun seeps through slatted roof shades, illuminating a million golden dust motes.

The main artery of the souks is **Souk Semmarine** (map F3), a broad, covered alley that begins with pottery and pâtisserie and moves into good quality fabric and textiles shops, selling everything from kaftans to pashminas, and huge, expensive, tourist emporiums full of antiques, carpets and jewellery. About halfway along, Souk Semmarine forks. On the right is **Spice Square** (p.40) and on the left is **Souk el Attarine**, bright and gleaming with copper and brass lanterns, mirrors, candlesticks, silver teapots and lamps, as well as spices and perfumes (for which it was traditionally known).

Souk Smata (map F4) is unmistakably the shoe souk, with brightly-coloured and sequined *babouches* (Moroccan slippers). Leading off Attarine is **Souk el Kebir** and **Souk Cherratin**, the preserve of leatherworkers and the place to go to buy bags, belts, wallets and purses. To the left of Souk el Kebir are the *kissarias*, covered souks selling clothing and fabrics. There are some great little

---

TIPS FOR HAGGLING
Don't ask the price of something unless you are willing to buy it. Be prepared to take your time. The general rule of thumb is to offer half of the seller's first price and go from there. There is never a 'correct price' – if you want something and are happy to pay the price, then you have paid the right amount.

shops here, too, with chic lanterns, glassware, baskets and antiques. To the right of Kebir is the jewellery souk, **Souk des Bijoutiers** (map F4). Nowhere is Morocco's living craftsmanship better illuminated than in the working carpenters' and blacksmiths' souks – **Souk Chouari** (map E4) and **Souk Haddadine** (map F4), at the northern edge of the souks. These fragrant, noisy alleys are refreshingly untouristy. To the southwest of this main cluster of streets is **Souk Sebbaghine** or **Souk des Teinturiers** (map E4) – the dyers souk, where rich iridescent skeins of wools and silks coloured with indigo, saffron, mint, poppy and rose blaze against the sky. Music lovers should explore **Souk Kimakhine** (map F4), where traditional Moroccan and Gnaoua instruments are sold.

Treat your senses to the **multicoloured delights** of **Spice Square**

The Rahba Kedima or **Spice Square** is bursting with magic. Nowhere is the fusion of Africa and Arabia that so characterizes Marrakech more apparent than in this vibrant, colourful, chaotic, ancient square.

Come here to buy all sorts of mysterious potions and lotions. For magic spells, there are live chameleons (if a chameleon thrown onto a fire explodes, your husband is having an affair), turtles, lizards, leopard and zebra skins, roots, barks, herbs, leaves, seeds, horns, tusks – cures for everything, from arthritis to a broken heart.

There are stalls selling herbal remedies, cosmetics and toiletries: cochineal powder for rouge, kohl, henna, natural crystal deodorant, herbal 'Viagra', toothbrushing twigs and essential oils of amber, musk, rose, patchouli and orange blossom.

For cookery lovers, there is a plethora of spices to choose from: saffron (ask for the good stuff under the counter), argan oil, ground cumin and coriander, shards of mace, star anis, rolls of cinnamon and home-made mixtures of spices created for marinading fish, fruit or meat.

In the middle of the square are piles of handmade baskets, wooden *harira* spoons, hats and pyramids of fruit and vegetables from the countryside. The old slave market, now the **Criée Berbère** *(p.50)*, is through a covered alley off the north side of the square and next to it is the gorgeous **Café des Epices**, where a sandwich costs around 30dh. Sit at wooden tables on the pavement, on the first floor surrounded by exhibits of art and photography or on the little roof terrace. Free Wi-fi.

Café des Epices; 75 Rahba Kedima; tel: 0524 391 770; B, L; map F3

Experience Ministero del Gusto – art gallery, design mecca, vintage boutique...

You won't know what's hit you when you step inside the mad, magical world that is **Ministero del Gusto**. Established in 1998 by Fabrizio Bizarri, a designer, and Alessandra Lippini, former fashion editor of Italian Vogue, Ministero del Gusto is a homage to their passion for the beautiful and the unusual in all things – from Italy to Africa, Pop Art to Art Deco, furniture to high fashion.

Behind an unassuming wooden door in the heart of the Mouassine area of the medina lies a dreamlike world that will delight art, design and fashion lovers. This is arguably one of the most cutting-edge, unconventional places in Morocco to shop, browse art and pick up a bit of inspiration.

The tribal sculptures and rough ochre walls of the courtyard are pure Africa; the leather bath fed with water from a tree trunk and the one-off pieces of furniture are pure fantasy; the eclectic art on the walls – from Pop Art-esque works by Hassan Hajjaj to photographs by Martin Schreiber – are windows onto every conceivable world, and Alessandra's dazzling vintage clothing and jewellery collection (think Pucci, Valentino, Versace, Dior, Hervé Leger and Chanel) will send fashionistas straight to heaven.

Everything you see is for sale, but for those who dream of extending their Marrakech experience through owning a place as enchanted as Ministero del Gusto, Alessandro and Fabrizio also renovate and design riads, houses and villas across Morocco.

Appointments advised.

Ministero del Gusto; 22 Derb Azzouz, Mouassine; tel: 0524 42 64 55; www. ministerodelgusto.com; map E4

Shop till you drop at all the best boutique shops in the medina

Exciting boutiques are springing up all over the medina. It's not just about the souks these days...

Atelier Moro (114 Place de Mouassine; map E4) is full of linen and silk kaftans, vintage carpets, 1920s ivory cigarette holders, glass perfume bottles and kitsch picture frames. **Akbar Delights** (Place Bab Fteuh; map E3) is so successful it now has shops in Paris and Rome. There are hand-embroidered kaftans and bejewelled slippers, beaded bags, Indian silk cushions and sculptures from West Africa. **Beldi** (9–11 Rue Mouassine; map E3) began as a tailor's in the 1940s

and is *the* place to go for haute couture: chic kaftans, velvet coats, vintage fabrics and jewellery.

Stéphanie Bénetière of **Kif Kif** (8 Rue el Ksour; map D3) employs Marrakchi artisans to create suede and leather bags, children's clothes, ethnic jewellery and home accessories. At **+Michi** (19–21 Souk Kchabbia; map E4), everyday items have been transformed into things that are fanciful and fun: handbags and *babouches* made out of flour sacks, hexagonal petrol tin coffee tables and one-off pieces of clothing. **Kulchi** (1 Rue el Ksour; map D3) sells raffia handbags and printed t-shirts by artist Hassan Hajjaj. **Au Fil d'Or** (10 Souk Semmarine; map E3) has snakeskin babouches, cashmere cloaks and fine cotton kaftans.

Some of the best boutiques are also non-profit. The **Coopérative Artisanale des Femmes de Marrakech** (67 Souk Kchabbia; map E4) sells cotton and linen clothing and household items. **Al-Kawtar** (57 Rue el Ksour; map E3) employs disabled women who fashion embroidered linen sheets and tablecloths, kaftans and dresses. **Assouss Coopérative d'Argan** (94 Rue Mouassine; map E4) sells cosmetics and salad oils made from argan.

Immerse yourself in **art and literature** at 15th-century riad **Dar Cherifa**

Riad-renovator extraordinaire Abdellatif Aït ben Abdallah's greatest work of art is 15th century **Dar Cherifa**, one of the oldest and most prestigious riads in the medina. Using only traditional materials and building techniques and employing master craftsmen, Abdallah ensured that Dar Cherifa remained authentic and faithful to the original house during its restoration.

Its simple grandeur – carved stucco and filigree woodwork, soaring whitewashed arches and delicate *zellige* tiling – is breathtaking. His intention was to revive the history of the house and promote Morocco's cultural heritage, taking inspiration from a previous 19th century owner, 'Fqih Jimmi', imam of the nearby Mouassine Mosque, who was a great patron of poetry and literature.

Today this extraordinary cultural heritage lives on through regular exhibitions of painting and sculpture by local and international artists; literary salons, cooking, calligraphy and ceramics workshops, and musical evenings with Gnaoua and Sufi musicians.

But even when no event is planned, Dar Cherifa should be on your list of places to see. Have tea on the beautiful roof terrace, browse a wonderful library of books on Morocco or have lunch here (on request, between noon and 4pm).

Dar Cherifa; 8 Derb Chorfa Lakbir; tel: 0524 42 64 63; daily 9am–7pm, L; map E3

Rise above it and **enjoy lunch** on a **roof terrace overlooking the medina**

After a morning spent battling through the souks, what better way to take a breather than by retreating to a breezy roof terrace for lunch?

One of the only places in the medina that has an alcohol license, **Café Arabe** is on the edge of the main souks. You can either sit under old orange trees in the blue courtyard or on the roof terrace, with incredible views over the medina, the Koutoubia and the High Atlas mountains. With an Italian/Moroccan menu that includes lasagne, tagine and *briouates* (stuffed pastries), this is one of the best places for lunch in the medina, with reasonable prices – around 300dh for two.

La Terrasse des Epices is round the corner and, though it doesn't serve alcohol, it has better food and a funky terrace. Giant woven lanterns hang like globes above you and low tables are surrounded by comfy seating for tired bodies. The food is delicious – the succulent chicken and beef brochettes, light lamb, date and almond tagines, crème brûlée and spiced canelle oranges will make you want to come back again for dinner. Expect to pay the same as Café Arabe.

Café Arabe; 184 Rue Mouassine;
tel: 0524 42 97 28; daily L, D; map E4
La Terrasse des Epices; 15 Souk Cherifia;
tel: 0524 37 59 04; daily L, D; map E4

Shop at a fabulous new **boutique collective** in the heart of the souks

Beneath Terraces des Epices, at the northern edge of the souks, is a shopping experience with a difference. **La Galerie** is a gorgeous split-level courtyard space that houses 15 quirky boutique shops which take the very best of Moroccan design – be that a lantern, a piece of jewellery or a kaftan – and work in modern twists that draw inspiration from around the world.

There is certainly nothing mundane here; it's all about one-off, bespoke pieces that you won't find anywhere else. **Stephanie Jewels** is a purveyor of beautifully delicate gold jewellery; **Alrazal** sells adorable silk and cotton children's clothes; **Original Marrakech** has straw baskets, hats, bottle-holders and lights all created by local women; **Florence D'Arabie** is a treasure trove of vintage, reclaimed and reworked objects; **Alhaia** has a lovely collection of tailored kaftans, cosy coats and elegant accessories; **Lalla**, the first shop to open here, is a favourite of fashionistas who flock here to buy Laetitia Trouillet's fantastic bags; **Kamal** sells beautiful china and glassware from La Terraces des Epices, children's toys, canvas bags and t-shirts designed by Hassan Hajjaj and José Levy, with profits going to ALCS which fights Aids in Marrakech; **Mergen Alaoui** is a scented paradise with locally-produced oriental perfumes of musk, amber, jasmine and vanilla as well as spa products, and **La Maison de Bahira** specializes in quality linen sheets, bedspreads, tunics and bathrobes – all created by Marion Théard, who started her career embroidering for Christian Louboutin.

La Galerie; 15 Souk Cherifia, Medina; map E4

Have a **sunlit lunch** and then wallow in a chic **plunge pool**

Marrakech is one of the best places in the world for decadent relaxation, with breezy roof terraces and shady courtyards to lounge about in, away from the heat of the sun and the chaos of the city. Many hotels allow non-guests to have lunch and use their pools too.

Riad el Fenn (Derb Moulay Abdullah ben Hezzian, Bab el Ksour; tel: 0524 44 12 10; map D3) is a bohemian yet luxurious boutique hotel. Lunch is fresh, light and made entirely from local produce. Eat on the roof terrace, which has a miniature putting green directed straight at the Koutoubia. If that sounds like too much activity, take advantage of the plunge pool with sun loungers, towels and Berber straw hats available. There is no charge on top of what you pay for lunch, and the spa and evening rooftop bar are both open to non-residents too.

Les Jardins de la Koutoubia (26 Rue de la Koutoubia; tel: 0524 38 88 00; map D2) is perfectly located right next to Jemaa el Fna. A grand hotel in the style of a huge riad, the elegant pool is shaded by palm trees, and lunch – club sandwiches, Dover sole, pasta – is very good value. There

is a 200dh charge per person, and the Clarins spa is also available for non-guests to use.

Sofitel (Rue Harroun Errachid; tel: 0524 42 56 00; map p.125 G1) and **Es Saadi** (Rue Ibrahim el Mazini; tel: 0524 44 88 11; map p.125 G1) in Hivernage also let you use their pools (for a fee), as does **Les Jardins de la Medina** (21 Derb Chtouka, Kasbah; tel: 0524 38 18 51; map p.56 C3) in the Southern Medina (free with lunch or a spa treatment).

Reservations are recommended at all of the above.

Sit outside **Café de France** and be inspired by Marrakech's **literary past**

Faded and unapologetically untouristy, **Café de France** on Jemaa el Fna is a Marrakech institution. It is a nostalgic reminder of the city's role as literary muse. Not all the writers who came to Marrakech spent time here, but as **Peter Mayne** wrote much of *A Year in Marrakesh* at one of these tables, it's as good a place as any to contemplate how Marrakech has inspired writers over the years.

Ibn Battuta, famous for his journeys spanning the entire Islamic world, visited Marrakech in the 14th century when the city was ravaged by plague, but still thought it one of the most beautiful places he had seen. In 1931 the artist **Wyndham Lewis** travelled around Morocco and wrote *Journey into Barbary*, a riveting portrait of the Berbers.

George Orwell came here on doctor's orders in the winter of 1938, stayed in a house in the Ville Nouvelle and wrote *Coming up for Air*, as well as an essay, *Marrakech*, on poverty and colonialism. In 1966, **Gavin Maxwell** spent time exploring the tumultuous lives of the powerful Glaoui family, whose ghosts still linger in parts of Marrakech, such as the Bahia Palace *(p.62)*. His book, *Lords of the Atlas*, was banned by King Hassan II as being subversive.

Esther Freud lived in Marrakech for nearly two years in the sixties when it was the epicentre of blissed-out hippiedom and paid homage to the city and the era in *Hideous Kinky*.

Café de France; Jemaa el Fna; daily B, L, D; map F2

Terrasse Panoramique

Res

47

Feast like a sultan at one of Marrakech's best **Moroccan restaurants**

Moroccan food is synonymous with luxurious feasting. In the past, sultans would spend hours eating course after course of intricate dishes that would have taken days to prepare. In spite of the huge amount of food and high prices to match, a traditional Moroccan feast should be at the top of any self-respecting gourmet's list of things to do in Marrakech.

Le Tobsil is considered by many (including Michael Winner) to be the best restaurant in town. Seating is in a candlelit courtyard or upper gallery. The exquisite food, conjured up by talented chef Fatima Mountassamim,

is traditional yet refined and includes flavoursome Moroccan salads, fragrant pigeon and almond *pastilla* (a flaky pastry pie dusted with icing sugar), lamb tagine with dates and fresh figs, chicken tagine with honey and apricots, and a milk *pastilla* with almonds and orange flower water.

Dar Moha dazzles in a different way. In what used to be fashion designer Pierre Balmain's house, owner and chef Mohammed Fedal whips up delectable Moroccan nouvelle cuisine. The dishes are recognisable but have subtle twists – cucumbers marinated in orange flower water, monkfish *pastilla*, foie gras couscous and quail tagine.

Though most definitely a feast, the emphasis at Dar Moha is on a multitude of taste experiences, rather than an overwhelmingly heavy meal. Ensure you reserve a table round the romantic, flower-strewn pool in the courtyard. Both restaurants are at the top end of the price scale (around 1,000dh for two people).

Le Tobsil; 22 Derb Abdallah ben Hessaien; tel: 0524 44 40 52; Wed-Mon L, D; map D2
Dar Moha; 81 Rue Dar el Bacha; tel: 0524 38 64 00; Tue-Sun L, D; map C4

Forget haggling and shop for arts and crafts at the price-set **Ensemble Artisanal**

Shopping in Marrakech's souks can be a frustrating and expensive experience. If you have had enough of endless haggling, head to the **Ensemble Artisanal**, which has a fantastic array of Moroccan arts and crafts – everything you find in the souk and more – and, best of all, every item has a price tag, which means there's no haggling required and none of the pestering that can accompany a shopping trip in the souk.

There are Ensemble Artisanals across Morocco; all are government-funded, and everything is made by local craftsmen or brought in from areas specializing in certain craft skills, such as jewellery or pottery. If there are several workshops selling the same thing, it's worth shopping around to make sure you're getting the best price.

Come here to pick up *tadelakt* (polished plaster) bowls and candle holders, terracotta tagines, brass and glass lanterns, carpets, silver Berber jewellery, *passementerie* key chains, leather bags, argan oil, ceramics from Fez and Safi, leather and silk pouffes, kaftans and jellabas. An added pleasure is being able to watch certain crafts being made. There are lantern-makers hammering out metal and carpet weavers at their looms. If you are interested, they will let you have a go.

Crafty shoppers should come here to check the price of common items and then brave the souks armed with a ballpark figure of what things cost; if you're good at haggling, you should pay less in the souks than at the Ensemble Artisanal.

Ensemble Artisanal; Avenue Mohammed V; tel: 0524 38 67 58; daily 9am–7pm; map B3

Sip mint tea with a carpet seller and listen to the tales he weaves

For many, a trip to Marrakech isn't complete without buying a carpet, or at least visiting a carpet shop. Moroccan carpets can be grouped into rural or urban, Berber or Arab. Urban carpets are influenced by the fine, oriental designs of the Middle East and are intricately detailed. Rural Berber carpets (arguably more interesting) are handwoven into abstract patterns and symbols that tell the stories of a tribe. Carpets from the Middle Atlas – *zanafi* – have a deep, woollen pile to keep out the cold and are usually long and narrow. The creamy *shedwi* carpets of the High and Middle Atlas Beni Ourain and Beni Mguild tribes are decorated with simple black or dark brown patterns. The *haouz* carpets of the west, between the Atlas and the Atlantic, have free-floating shapes and bright colours. **Kilims**, or *hanbels*, from Chichaoua, are flat-woven rugs with detailed geometric designs and usually coloured in black, white and yellow on a red background.

Berber carpets – with their unique, irreverent, free designs – are informal and fun and tend to work well in modern, western surroundings. As such, certain types of Moroccan carpet – the Beni Ourain and Beni Mguild in particular – have recently become the height of fashion in the west.

The art of carpet weaving is exclusively female and influenced by pre-Islamic beliefs that are entrenched in magic and the legends of the Berber tribes. Traditionally, carpets were made solely for personal use. This means that every symbol, motif and pattern means something special to the weaver – perhaps a wish for fertility, the celebration of a marriage or birth, or an ode to the landscape of a particular region. When you buy a Moroccan carpet, therefore, you are buying a talisman and a unique story.

One of the best places to buy carpets is in the **Criée Berbère** (Berber auction; map F3) off the Spice Square – the entrance is flanked by two outdoor carpet stalls. Slave auctions were held here three times a week at sunset, a practice that continued until the French arrived in 1912. Today, the only auctions are for wool, cloth and carpets.

The Criée Berbère is an exotic covered warren of dozens of small carpet shops. All are pretty much the same and if the shop you choose doesn't have something you want, the owner will just borrow one from a neighbouring shop that does.

If you are serious about buying a carpet, you must be prepared to spend some time here, choosing what you want and negotiating the price. This is a delicate art, requiring patience, humour and a lot of mint tea. A good carpet seller will be able to tell you the intricate stories behind the patterns and motifs, making your buying experience all the more enjoyable. If you immerse yourself in the process, and stick to your budget, you will walk away not only with a carpet that you love and that didn't cost the earth, but also with an authentic, unique piece of Moroccan folklore.

Ben Rahal, in Guéliz (map on p.104, D3), also has one of the finest collections of carpets in town.

Splurge on an **unforgettable evening** at the magical **Royal Mansour**

There are hotels and then there are hotels. The **Royal Mansour**, passionate project of King Mohammed VI, is a celebration of the very best in Moroccan design and craftsmanship and unquestionably one of the most opulent hotels in the world. No expense was spared in its creation, which took four years and involved thousands of Moroccan artisans. This is a place where fantasy and beauty rule. Entry is gained through a suitably regal four-ton bronze doorway and in winter a fire roars in a floor-to-ceiling glass chimney. The wonderfully moody cigar bar has black and gold enamel walls and the wood-panelled library has a retracting roof and telescope for star-gazing.

Accommodation is in 53 individual riads, each with roof terrace plunge pool and 24-hour butler. Like something out of James Bond, underground tunnels enable staff to move around without disturbing guests. There is also a spa (which non-guests can use), a children's club and an art gallery.

Best of all, the food. Supervised by 3 star Michelin chef, Yannick Alléno, there are two restaurants: **La Grande Table Marocaine**, serving Moroccan specialities, and **La Grande Table Française** – said to be the best French restaurant in Africa. Eating here isn't cheap, but for foodies and anyone who wants to catch a glimpse of this glorious hotel, it is well worth it. Make sure you have a pre-dinner cocktail in the breathtaking Martini Bar.

Royal Mansour; Rue Abou el Abbas Sebti; tel: 0529 80 80 80; daily L, D; map A2

Eat a mouthwatering **Marrakchi speciality**... slow roast lamb

Moroccan food isn't just about tagine and couscous. *Méchoui* (the word comes from the Arabic *sawa*, which means 'roasted on a fire') is a succulent, crispy, intensely-flavoured slow roast lamb that is a speciality of North African cuisine. In Morocco, the lamb is heavily spiced and then suspended whole (including head, skin and organs) in a clay underground oven and cooked for an entire day, during which the meat is slowly turned and basted in butter.

Traditionally, *méchoui* was prepared for special occasions, such as weddings, where guests of honour would be served the choicest bits (the eyes, grain-filled intestines, cheeks), but these days it can also be found in a few spots in the medina. **Méchoui Alley** (map F2) just off the northern edge of Jemaa el Fna, is one of the best-kept foodie secrets in Marrakech and a place full of locals but very few tourists. Come here in the evening and you will be treated to one of the most delicious street food meals you'll ever eat. Place your order and the chef will remove the lamb from the oven, tear off a few select chunks, fling it onto a plate or some paper, sprinkle it with salt and cumin and serve it with a hunk of fresh bread. Be prepared to get messy – eating *méchoui* should only be done with your fingers, for maximum flavour impact, and to show how easily the meat falls off the bone.

Southern Medina

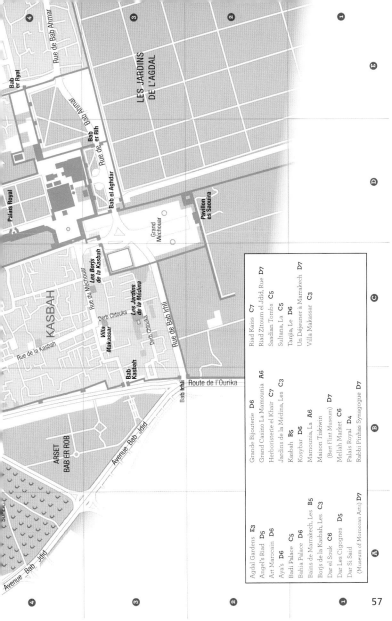

LES JARDINS DE L'AGDAL

Palais Royal

Grand Mechouar

Pavillon es Saouira

KASBAH

Les Borjs de la Kasbah

Villa Makassar

Les Jardins de la Medina

Bab el Aghdar

Bab er Ryal

Rue de Bab Ahmar

Rue de er Rih

Rue du Mechouar

Rue de la Kasbah

Derb Chtouka

Bab Kasbah

Rue de Bab Irhil

Bab Irhil

Route de l'Ourika

ARSET BAB ER ROB

Avenue Bab-Jdid

Watch **Aladdin's lamp** being made at **Place des Ferblantiers**

The **Place des Ferblantiers** ('Ironmongers' Square'; map D6) is a fantastically animated square wedged in between the **Mellah** (Jewish Quarter) and **Kasbah**.

Dozens of workshops line this pretty pedestrian space; inside, ironworkers hammer out the intricate lanterns for which Morocco is famous. Hanging from every hook and laid out in front of each workshop are hundreds of their creations: multi-coloured glass, elegant nickel-plated, dramatic iron and copper that has been punctured into delicate filigree. For anyone wanting to buy their very own Aladdin's lamp, this is the place to come. You will pay less here than you would in the main souks and there is the added advantage of seeing the lamp being made and knowing that your money will go directly to the person who made it. Many workshops will make lamps to order.

As you enter the square from Avenue Houmman el Fetouaki, there are a couple of simple but good tagine restaurants on the right-hand side. Don't be put off by the ramshackle nature of these places – the tagines (cooked on outdoor grills) and simple kefta sandwiches are delicious. To the left, there is a quirkily inventive shop where everything is made out of colourful sardine tins.

The southern edge of the square, where you'll find two popular cafés, **Kosybar** and **Le Tanjia** (p.60), leads on to the **Badi Palace** (p.74). Just before this exit, there is an art gallery-cum-shop, **Art Marocain**, which has interesting modern Moroccan paintings for sale.

Art Marocain; 50 Place des Ferblantiers; daily 9am–8pm; map D6

Indulge your inner Talitha Getty at **the best kaftan shops in town**

The kaftan, an iconic piece of clothing that was the uniform of choice for bohemians in the 1960s and '70s (think Patrick Lichfield's legendary photograph of Talitha Getty lounging glamorously on a Marrakech rooftop), has experienced a 21st-century revival as boho-chic holiday clothing.

In Morocco, the kaftan is the traditional dress for women; it can be a simple piece of cotton or wool that is worn everyday or a breathtakingly sumptuous work of art that is brought out only on special occasions. Most women still have their kaftans tailor-made, which means you will find tailors and fabric shops in every quarter of the medina.

For those wanting something with a modern edge, **Aya's** is one of the most exclusive kaftan shops in the medina. Nawal al Hriti, the owner and designer, produces exquisitely made hand-stitched and embroidered kaftans and tunics of silk, cashmere and linen in every colour, pattern and style imaginable (for men and kids, too). Inspired by traditional designs, but with modern lines, every piece is a one-off and Nawal also offers a bespoke tailoring service and can produce a kaftan in 3–4 days

if she doesn't have many other orders. Prices start from around £100 for something off-the-peg. She also sells antique postcards of Marrakech, semi-precious jewellery, throws and cushions, babouches and bags. Aya's also now stocks the must-have kaftans from **Kazbek**, which used to be on Rue Riad Zitoun el Jdid.

Beldi (*p.42*) in the central medina, **Nour Kaftan** in the northern medina (212 Derb Sidi Bou Amar, Riad Larous), **Kaftan Queen** and **Michèle Baconnier** in Guéliz (both p.108) also have wonderful original kaftans.

Aya's; 11 Derb Jdid Bab Mellah (just before Place des Ferblantiers); map D6

Rock the kasbah – at Kosybar, where jazz mingles with the evening prayer

a table on the gorgeous roof terrace, in time to watch the sun fizzle over the medina rooftops. The bar serves great cocktails and the hip restaurant offers delicious Asian-influenced food prepared by Japanese chef, Nao Tamaki. A main course costs from around 100dh.

The owners of Kosybar are part of Morocco's biggest wine-producing family, which explains the interesting wine list. Most evenings there is good live jazz and blues playing downstairs.

Next door is the equally popular restaurant **Le Tanjia**, an 'oriental brasserie' in yet another delightful old riad (with prices which are just a little higher than Kosybar). Seating is on two levels around the pretty courtyard or on the roof terrace, and the menu is a mixture of European and Moroccan, including the namesake dish *tanjia* – richly-flavoured lamb cooked for several hours (usually in the fire of a hammam) in a covered clay pot.

One of the only bars in the medina, **Kosybar** is brilliantly situated on the edge of the Place des Ferblantiers in a wonderful 19th century riad, with lavish Moroccan-Asian interiors. Adjoining the walls of the Badi Palace, Kosybar has as its neighbours dozens of storks, which are considered a great sign of *baraka*, or luck, to Muslims. At sunset the unusual sound of their clashing bills mixes exotically with the evening call to prayer.

Kosybar is a good spot for lunch, but the most popular time is in the evening, when it becomes lively with expats and tourists. Come early to bag

Kosybar; 47 Place des Ferblantiers; tel: 0524 38 03 24; daily until 1am L, D; map D6
Le Tanjia; 14 Derb Jdid; tel: 0524 38 38 36; daily L, D; map D6

60

Discover the world of **traditional herbal medicine** at an **apothecary**

For fans of holistic natural remedies and cosmetics the apothecaries of Morocco are tantalizing places to visit. These traditional pharmacies are great fun to explore; as well as learning a bit about the medicinal and cosmetic properties of various plants, herbs and oils, you can buy pampering products or unusual gifts. Essential oils, perfumes and spices are all great things to take home as fragrant reminders of your trip.

This is also where you can pick up a bottle of **argan oil**. Made from the nut of a tree grown only in southern Morocco, argan is superfood, anti-ageing miracle and medicine rolled into one. It has twice as much vitamin E as olive oil, is rich in antioxidants and contains omega 6. Used by Moroccans for centuries as a flavouring and cosmetic (an Egyptian botanist in the 13th century first noted its health-giving properties), it has only recently been discovered in the west.

Herboristerie el Khair is a family-run company whose knowledge of 'the art of plants' has been handed down through successive generations to the current owner. Abdelatif Akhdar speaks English and can prepare bespoke aromatherapy oils, organic perfumes and spice mixtures. His wonderful shop is lined floor to ceiling with glass jars full of hundreds of spices, herbs, nuts and seeds, including natural cosmetics, medicinal teas, incense, dried lavender and rosebuds...

For those who prefer the herbal approach to health and beauty, this is the perfect one-stop shop.

Herboristerie el Khair; 71 Rue Riad Zitoun Jdid; map C7

Be bewitched by the **sun-dappled courtyards** of the **Bahia Palace**

The **Bahia Palace** (Palais el Bahia) literally translates as 'the beautiful' and is unique in Morocco as the only royal palace that can be visited. Here you sense how life used to be lived in the days of sultans and courtiers, intrigues, political plots and, of course, extremes of extravagance.

The Bahia was built in the 1860s by Si Moussa, Grand Vizier (a powerful political advisor) to Sultan Sidi Mohamed Ben Abderrahman, and expanded in the late 1800s by Abu 'Bou' Ahmed, also a Grand Vizier. The latter was the son of an African palace slave but became one of the most powerful men in Morocco when Moulay Abdul Aziz was sultan. According to the Times journalist, Walter Harris,

Bou Ahmed was, 'a man of no particular intelligence, but of indomitable will, and cruel.' The entire palace took 14 years to build and involved hundreds of the best artisans in Morocco; it is a palace more than fit for a king, attesting to the tremendous wealth and stature of both Si Moussa and Bou Ahmed. Bou Ahmed lived in the Bahia with his four wives and 24 concubines – the empty and, therefore, surprisingly stark harem can still be seen, as can the vast, open-air, marble-paved 'Court of Honour' surrounded by a carved wooden gallery, where citizens would gather to be heard by the vizier or be handed out draconian punishments.

The Bahia is an extraordinary display of the finest Moroccan craftsmanship and skill, and an example of the period's post-Alhambra style decoration. The series of gardens, once-luxurious apartments, courtyards and cool reception halls, with their intricate *zellige* floors, painted cedar ceilings, finely carved stucco, and huge carved and painted wooden doors are breathtaking.

When Bou Ahmed died, his once-loyal staff and even his wives and courtesans looted and pillaged the palace, taking everything they could and stripping much of the interiors of their ornament. In the early 20th century, Thami el Glaoui, the notorious warlord and Pasha of Marrakech, used the Bahia as one of his residences and held lavish parties here. When the French Protectorate was established in 1912, Glaoui was evicted and the Governor used it as his main residence. Today it is officially part of the Royal Palace and parts of it, including most of the upstairs rooms, are used by King Mohammed VI for lodging guests. Jackie and Aristotle Onassis once stayed here and hip hop mogul Sean Combs held an extravagant birthday party in the palace in 2002. In total, the Bahia gardens cover 8 hectares and there are a total of 150 rooms, only a fraction of which can be seen by the public.

Bahia Palace; Rue Riad Zitoun el Jdid; daily 8.45–11.45am, 2.45–5.45pm, Fri 8.30–11.30am, 3–5.45pm; charge; map D6

Make like a Sultana and float away at
Les Bains de Marrakech

The art of pampering is long-established in Morocco and stems from the traditional Moroccan bath, or **hammam** *(p.98)*. Marrakech is full of spas to indulge yourself, and no trip to the city is complete without at least one visit. Many hotels and guesthouses have hammams and spas or will be able to arrange for a visit to one nearby.

One of the best spas is **Les Bains de Marrakech**, a riad in the kasbah that is entirely devoted to luxurious indulgence. This serene place – all muted colours, warm wood, candles and exotic scents – is a blissful escape.

A bonus of this spa is that you can go as a couple. There are joint massage cabins, steam baths with exotic oriental treatments such as sea salt body scrub with geranium and grapefruit and mint essential oil body wrap

and hammams where you'll be steamed, soaped and scrubbed to within an inch of your life. The massages are all tailored and include Shiatsu, the delicious-sounding 'chocolate Zen', a four-handed synchronized oil massage and hot stone therapy. Argan facials and milk and honey manicures and pedicures are also available. All products used are 100% natural.

'Day spa' packages of three treatments start at 800dh and an hour's massage starts at 350dh per person. Tailored packages are also available, as well as full 'return to fitness' plans on request.

Book at least two weeks in advance.

Les Bains de Marrakech; 2 Derb Sedra; tel: 0524 38 14 28; www.lesbainsde marrakech.com; daily 9am–8pm; B5

Wander around **foodie heaven** in the **Mellah Market**

The food markets of Morocco are largely overshadowed by their more exotic sisters, the souks, but unjustifiably so. Whether it is a small rural market or something far larger, these markets are where Moroccans come to shop, catch up with gossip, flirt and do business. This is where the real life of Morocco is played out—something that can be lacking in many places more geared to tourism.

The **Mellah Market**, in the eponymous Jewish quarter of the medina, is one of the oldest in Marrakech. The *mellahs* were ghettoes sectioned off from the rest of the city where the Jewish population lived, and the market was a lifeline for the quarter. Though the Mellah is no longer a ghetto and most of the Jews who lived here have left, there are still reminders of its past in a couple of kosher butchers.

As you enter the huge covered space, you are assailed by the scent of roses, vegetables and fresh meat. The flowers cascade from stalls just inside the entrance; opposite are a couple of butchers selling legs of lamb, merguez sausages, chickens and beef. Beyond, there are vegetable stalls with fresh, organic and seasonal produce piled like edible jewels. Still further, there are stalls selling preserved lemons, onions and cucumbers, spices, herbs and olives marinated in a thousand different ways. There is a spice auction every day at 4pm in this section of the market. In addition to food, there are whole areas devoted to the selling of fabrics and two large old fondouks (craftsmen's workshops) that now mainly deal in traditional cosmetics and medicinal herbs.

Mellah Market; off Avenue Houmman el Fetouaki; closed Fri; C6

Step into the **Saadian Tombs** – an afterlife fantasy that rivals the Taj Mahal

The great Saadian dynasty (1509–1659) ushered in a golden age for Morocco. The Saadians emerged from the Drâa Valley during the 16th century and, on a wave of religious fervour and nationalist sentiment, swept through the country, making Marrakech their capital in 1524. They reached the pinnacle of their wealth and power under Ahmed el Mansour, 'the Victorious' (1578–1603), who built the **Badi Palace** (p.74) and the **Saadian Tombs** (Tombeaux Saadiens).

The Saadian Tombs were built on the site of an older cemetery reserved for descendants of the Prophet. After the collapse of the dynasty, the tombs were bricked up in the late 17th century by Moulay Ismail, who destroyed Badi Palace but out of superstition left the tombs intact; they were only rediscovered by a French aerial survey of the medina in 1917.

The two main mausoleums consist of 66 tombs inside and a further 100 outside in the gardens. Of the two, Ahmed el Mansour's mausoleum – with its soaring vaulted roof, intricate carved stucco and cedar wood detail and *zellige* tiling – is the most beautiful. Both are stylistic echoes of the Alhambra in Granada, which was built 200 years earlier. The first marble-floored hall of Mansour's mausoleum houses the tombs of several Saadians, including the 'mad' sultan, Moulay Yazid. At the back, is the stunning hall of twelve columns, where the tomb of el Mansour is found.

To appreciate the beauty and peace of the tombs, it is best to visit in the early morning, before 10am.

Saadian Tombs; off Rue de la Kasbah; daily 8.30-11.45am, 2.30-5.45pm; charge; map C5

Escape to an oasis in the heart of the medina by staying at **a riad with a pool**

A traditional riad hotel in the medina, suffused with history and illuminating traditional Moroccan living, is an unmissable element of any stay and a riad with a pool is an added bonus. There is little more pleasurable than sinking into a shaded courtyard pool or having a rooftop dip at sunset.

You will be treated like royalty in the super-luxe **La Sultana**, which consists of five historic riads. The focal point is the elegant pool, which is heated and ionized and surrounded by the brick walls of the neighbouring Saadian Tombs. Swimming here is about as exotic as it gets and the spa is one of the best in town.

Les Borjs de la Kasbah, situated yards from the Royal Palace, took craftsmen four years to build and is blissfully tranquil. The pool is placed apart from the main courtyard, is heated in winter and there is a lovely little poolside bar serving cocktails and light summer food for lunch.

Once the harem of Sultan Moulay Yacoub, **Riad Kaiss** is one of longest established riad hotels in Marrakech and has also appeared in more design magazines than most. Although the courtyard with its jungly plants and tinkling fountain is wonderfully inviting, the chic little plunge pool on the roof terrace is the best draw, and with just nine rooms, you'll probably have it all to yourself.

La Sultana; 403 Rue de la Kasbah; tel: 0524 38 80 08; map C5
Les Borjs de la Kasbah; Rue du Méchouar; tel: 0524 38 11 01; map C3
Riad Kaiss; 65 Derb Jdid; Rue Riad Zitoun el Kdim; tel: 0524 44 01 41; map C7

Have a picnic under an olive tree in the Agdal Gardens

On summer Sundays hundreds of Marrakchi families head to the **Agdal Gardens** for a favourite Moroccan pastime: picnicking. In Islam, gardens are earthly suggestions of paradise – it was this romantic promise that drew artists such as Matisse and Delacroix to Morocco.

The vast Agdal Gardens (agdal means 'walled meadow' in Berber), were first created as an orchard in the 12th century; renovated by the Saadians in the 16th century and expanded into their present form by Alaouite Sultan Moulay Abderrahmane in the 19th century. Now a Unesco World Heritage Site, they include hundreds of olive trees as well as pomegranate, fig, orange, lemon and apricot trees. They are irrigated using tanks and a system of channels feeding water from the High Atlas through the groves. At the end of the largest tank – the Sahraj el Sana (Tank of Health) – is the Dar el Hana, built for the sultan to entertain his guests. Another pavilion, the Dar el Beida, was built by Sultan Moulay Hassan to house his harem.

Although cooking a tagine from scratch on a butane stove might be a stretch for most visitors, many riads will happily prepare a picnic lunch. Alternatively, pick up a sandwich or an ice cream from a nearby café, set yourself down beneath an old olive tree and imagine sultans and their entourage doing this before you (albeit more lavishly).

Agdal Gardens; Fri and Sun only 9am–sunset; map E3

Glimpse **the legacy of Jewish Marrakech** in the cemetery and synagogue of the Mellah

Established since the 3rd century, Judaism is the oldest religious denomination to have survived without interruption in Morocco to the present day. However, of the 300,000 Jews in the country before the founding of Israel in 1948, only a few thousand remain. There is a Jewish quarter *(mellah)* in every Moroccan city, which was always built close to the palace so that it should benefit from royal protection. The **Marrakech Mellah** was created in 1558 and is the second oldest in Morocco, after Fez.

The **cemetery** *(miâara)* and **Rabbi Pinhas synagogue** – largely overlooked by tourists – are poignant markers of a time that has faded into the past. The cemetery is the largest in Morocco – the original graves date back several centuries, with newer additions layered above. An Arab family lives within the cemetery and act as guardians

and caretakers. Theoretically, only Jews are allowed entry, but if you are respectful, they will let you in and show you around for a small tip. It is a serene place to visit in the late afternoon. The synagogue is the oldest in Marrakech, built in 1492 by Spanish Jews escaping the Inquisition. An ageing rabbi still lives there and will show you the peaceful blue and white courtyard and prayer hall. A small donation is requested.

Rabbi Pinhas synagogue;
Rue Talmud Torah; map D6

FESTIVAL OF EID

The Jewish faith's Abraham is one of Islam's most important prophets – Ibrahim – and it is in memory of Ibrahim's willingness to sacrifice his son that Muslims sacrifice a sheep every year to mark the festival of Eid el Kebir, following Ramadan.

Enjoy an **old-fashioned cocktail** at the Churchill Bar of **La Mamounia**

La Mamounia is one of the most famous hotels in the world, 'the Dorchester of North Africa' and, once upon a time, the life and soul of Marrakech. The grounds date back to the 18th century, when the Alaouite Sultan Sidi Mohammed Ben Abdallah gave the gardens as a wedding gift to his son, Mamoun, who used them for glamorous garden parties. La Mamounia opened as a hotel in 1923 – a dazzling example of superior Moroccan craftsmanship and elegant Art Deco design. The hotel has just reopened after an ambitious three-year, multi-million dollar redesign by Jacques Garcia, of Hotel Costes in Paris fame.

The atmospheric Churchill Bar (the only part of the hotel that wasn't renovated) is the best place to soak up some of La Mamounia's nostalgic old-school glamour. Sipping on your perfectly-mixed Martini, you can't help but wonder what secrets the wood-panelled walls have absorbed over the years. Did Churchill himself once recline in that corner, wreathed in cigar smoke? Did Mick Jagger and Keith Richards lounge on the leopard-print? Was this once where everyone from Omar Sharif to Franklin D. Roosevelt and Charlie Chaplin to Hitchcock used to let loose, swinging to the jazz piano? La Mamounia is steeped in history: part rock-and-roll, part Arabian Nights, part hippy haze, part gilded royalty.

Unusually, you don't have to stay here to get a little hit. Come for afternoon tea and afterwards wander around the spectacular gardens. Two hundred year-old olives as tall as oak trees tower over immaculate lawns and scented gardens bursting with roses, Barbary figs, Madagascar periwinkles, amaranths and agaves. Winston Churchill thought these gardens were the 'loveliest spot in the whole world'. There is also an organic vegetable garden with peach, orange, fig and lime trees and

> **LA MAMOUNIA'S SPA**
> La Mamounia's award-winning Wellness Spa has to be one of the most decadent in the world. Situated in what seems like its very own palace, with soaring columns, glimmering marble and giant oriental lanterns, if you need a little escape this is the place. There are several massage cabins, two hammams, an indoor ozone pool and a relaxation room, and the treatments include Shiseido and traditional Moroccan therapies.

everything here is used at the three Michelin-supervised restaurants. Make a reservation for dinner at **L'Italien**, **Le Français** or **Le Marocain**. All three are situated in wonderfully opulent surroundings and combine the best traditions of each cuisine with modern twists – chicken tagine with walnuts, semolina and caramelized pear at Le Marocain; lobster fritters with greens from the Mamounia garden at L'Italien and homemade lasagne with oxtail compote at Le Français.

Alternatively, head to the slightly more relaxed Le Pavillon de la Piscine, which is open for breakfast and a 'Mediterranean buffet' lunch.

Nothing at La Mamounia comes cheap, but if you possibly can, save up and treat yourself. Dress up in your chicest kaftan and pay homage to the grand old lady of Marrakech.

Reservations essential.

La Mamounia; Avenue Bab Jdid; tel: 0524 38 86 00; B, L, D; map A6

71

Admire the finest **Moroccan craftsmanship** at **Dar Si Said**

the legacy of Morocco's master craftsmen.

The ground floor exhibits stunning carved cedar doors, delicate *mashrabiya* screens and wonderful inlaid daggers and other weaponry. On the first and second floors are salons showcasing traditional life. Here you will find the precursors to everything you see in the souks: vintage kaftans, Berber jewellery, embroidered leather bags and saddles, intricate furniture, carpets from the High Atlas and Deep South, pottery, brass and silverware, including kettles with a compartment for burning the charcoal, conical-lidded containers intended for bread, long-spouted vessels for pouring water over the hands of dinner guests, and incense holders – the latter two essential preludes and postscripts to any elaborate meal in a traditional household to this day.

Occasionally, the museum will hold exhibitions of modern art, which contrast brilliantly with the antiques on display.

Not only is **Dar Si Said** (the **Museum of Moroccan Arts**) one of the most beautiful old palaces in Marrakech, it also houses one of the most fascinating collections of antique Moroccan art and craftsmanship in the world. Built in the 19th century by Si Said, the brother of Bou Ahmed, who also built the Bahia Palace (*p.62*), it was turned into a museum in the 1950s.

Come here to admire much-imitated Moroccan design and extremely fine architecture, both of which are outstandingly preserved in this celebration of

Dar Si Said; Derb el Bahia, Rue Riad Zitoun el Jdid; tel: 0524 38 95 64; Wed-Mon 9am-noon and 3-6pm; charge; map D7

Explore the **boutique souk shops** along **Rue Riad Zitoun el Jdid**

Rue Riad Zitoun el Jdid (Street of the New Olive Garden) is one of the most vibrant streets in the medina, with a mix of classic souk shops selling handblown tea glasses and slippers, and a scattering of more westernised boutiques. Start from Jemaa el Fna and work your way down.

El Louami Ahmed has unusual raffia shoes and *babouches*: some dramatically curled at the toe, others striped in a rainbow of colours. If Louami doesn't have your size or a style that you want, he'll make it for you. **Warda la Mouche** creates beautifully made cotton beach kaftans, metallic sandals, funky bags and luxury velvet evening kaftans. Each piece is unique and the prices won't break the bank.

Jamade specialises in bright ceramics – tagine pots, soap dishes, teapots, giant plates and tumblers – by local designers and women's cooperatives. Music lovers must visit the unnamed **Gnaoua music shop** (just follow your ears). Spilling out onto the street are dozens of Moroccan musical instruments for sale as well as albums by local and African artists that you won't find elsewhere. When you've shopped till you've dropped, have lunch at **Un Déjeuner à Marrakech**, where charming staff will whip up scrumptious things like beef stroganoff, caprese salad, vegetable tart, spinach and ricotta pie and tarte au citron. There is a little terrace with great views, too.

Un Déjeuner à Marrakech; 2–4 Place Douar Graoua, Rue Riad Zitoun el Jdid; tel: 0524 37 83 87; B, L, D (closes 8pm); map D7

Imagine bygone days when sultans ruled in the **Badi Palace**

The **Badi Palace** (Palais el Badi), which translates as 'the Incomparable' and is also one of the 99 names given to Allah in the Qur'an, was once a palace of outstanding beauty. Today, all that remains are the haunting ruins, but it is still an incredibly atmospheric place to visit, particularly in the late afternoon when the sun casts deep shadows across the russet pisé walls and you can conjure up ghosts of the past, when the palace was inhabited by the sultan, his harem and opulent court.

The palace was built in the 16th century by the Saadian sultan, Ahmed el Mansour – the greatest of all the Saadian rulers and a powerful and influential leader with a huge army who held sway in Europe's political struggles during the Renaissance period. A glittering symbol of Morocco's power and prestige, the palace was said to have been lavishly decorated with white Italian marble and Sudanese gold.

The palace took 25 years to build but, at the hands of Alaouite sultan Moulay Ismail less than a century later, just 12 years to destroy when he broke it down and took all the precious materials to build his own magnificent palace in Meknes.

The bulk of the Badi is an enormous open courtyard that follows traditional Islamic principles, with four huge sunken gardens filled with olive trees and a fountain in the centre. In the case of the Badi, there is a large rectangular pool with two grand pavilions at either end. Traces of the underground system that watered the garden still remain. Around the courtyard were 360 narrow rooms on two floors and beyond are the ruins of the old stables and a series of dungeons that were used right up to the 20th century as a prison. Efforts are underway to restore parts of the Badi, such as the courtyard pavilions, which house the original *minbar* from the Koutoubia Mosque, from which the imam would lead the faithful in prayer.

Badi Palace; Kasbah; daily 8.30–11.45am, 2.30–5.45pm; charge; map C5

Be dazzled by a world of **gold and silver jewellery** at the **Grande Bijouterie**

The art of the goldsmith is an ancient one. In virtually every major city in the world there were guilds of Jewish goldsmiths, and in every Jewish quarter an area was reserved for the craft of making gold and silver jewellery. In Marrakech, this trade continued right up until the middle of the 20th century. The **Grande Bijouterie**, which is found at the entrance to the Mellah, has only a few Jewish goldsmiths remaining, but this dazzling covered market is still an animated, fully functioning jewellery souk.

The jewellery in the Bijouterie is unlike anything you'll find in the rest of Marrakech, which is largely ethnic Berber and which most urban Moroccan women wouldn't be seen dead wearing. This is serious 'bling' jewellery, the glitzier the better. You'll see heavy gold-plated necklaces, bracelets and belts worn over kaftans at weddings, and slightly simpler silver pieces inset with semi-precious stones. Delicate filigree rings and bracelets contrast with these, and there are plenty of engraved silver hands of Fatima (a sign of good luck to both Jews and Arabs).

Regardless of whether or not you are in the market for some gold or silver jewellery, a meander through the brightly lit arcades is well worth doing – you may even spot pieces in the making (one of the great excitements in Morocco is seeing things being made in the shops in which they are sold). If you are looking to buy, make sure you know the value of gold and silver as everything here is priced on weight.

Grande Bijouterie; Rue Bab Mellah; daily 9.30am–8pm; D6

Travel from Marrakech to Timbuktu at
Maison Tiskiwin

The **Bert Flint Museum at Maison Tiskiwin** is one of the most inspiring yet least visited places in Marrakech. If there is one museum you choose to visit in the city, make it this one. Bert Flint, a veteran Dutch anthropologist and explorer, first came to Morocco in 1957 and has spent more than 50 years exploring and researching the culture and artistic heritage of this part of North Africa.

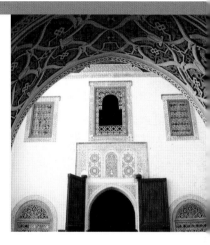

Maison Tiskiwin is his beautiful 19th century home which he transformed into an enlightening exhibition space for Moroccan and Saharan African arts and crafts. The lines between where the house ends and the museum begins are wonderfully blurred – you sense that no other museum will ever quite live up to this.

As well as celebrating simple beauty, the collection illuminates the links between Morocco and sub-Saharan Africa – a connection that is the very essence of Marrakech.

Everything here is arranged geographically. On cultural caravan tracks you trace Flint's journeys across southern Morocco, into Mali and Mauritania and on to Timbuktu. It is impossible not to be swept into the past, visualising the tribal and nomadic ways of life that mingled along the trans-Saharan caravan routes. Everything is a feast for the eyes: Tuareg artefacts, masks from Mali, an entire Berber tent made from camel hair, antique engraved guns, sculptural wooden spoons, dyed and patterned leather saddle bags, wicker mats from Mauritania, fabrics and textiles, musical instruments... Fittingly, everything has been bequeathed to the people of Morocco, through the Musée de Marrakech (p.86).

Maison Tiskiwin; 8 Derb el Bahia; daily 9am-12.30pm and 3-5.30pm; charge; map D7

Spend a **peaceful morning** at the breathtaking **Madrassa Ben Youssef**

With the exoticism and westernised glamour of luxury hotels, spas, shops and restaurants, it is sometimes easy to forget that Marrakech is an Islamic city and one that is also considered to be a holy pilgrimage site.

The lynchpin of daily life is still the mosque, and much basic learning focuses on the Qur'an, which was traditionally taught at a madrassa (religious school). A spectacular remnant of this is the **Madrassa Ben Youssef**. Religious reminders aside, it is also one of the most dazzling examples of Moorish architecture in the world, reminiscent of the Alhambra in Granada and the Alcázar in Seville.

The madrassa was founded during the Merinid era in the 14th century and reconstructed by the Saadians in the 16th century, who expanded it to become the largest madrassa in Morocco in a deliberate attempt to snub the imams of Fez (the spiritual heartland of the country). The madrassa closed down as a school in 1960 and, after restoration, opened to the public in 1982.

The entrance is unremarkable – just another wooden door on a medina street – but it serves to enhance the visual impact upon entering the main courtyard, where a jade green tiled rectangular pool reflects shining marble, carved cedar wood, lace-like stucco, scalloped archways and a blue rectangle of sky above. After the rough-edged chaos and noise of the streets outside, the madrassa is an unexpectedly elegant and refined sanctuary. The courtyard leads to a domed prayer hall, richly decorated with flowing Qur'anic inscriptions, *zellige* tilework and the most incredibly intricate stucco ceilings, looking more like stalactites in a white cave. In accordance with the laws of Islam, none of the decorations can depict animals or humans – everything is of a geometric design. Most guides (if you are with one) will encourage you to stand inside the prayer niche here and say something loud to illustrate the remarkable echo created – especially useful for a mullah with the 900 students that were said to have studied here at any one time. Lessons would revolve around learning the Qur'an by heart and on Islamic law and the sciences. Most students would go on to become mullahs, judges or lawyers.

On the first floor are the crumbling remains of 130 tiny dormitory cells – this is a particularly atmospheric part of the madrassa. Sneak away from the crowds to explore the dusty warren of rooms – some so tiny that you have to crouch low to enter, some of which afford tantalising glimpses into the courtyard below.

Come in the morning, when all is hushed and serene and the early sun highlights the exquisitely disciplined beauty of the place. If you are lucky, you might chance upon a young calligrapher who sometimes sets up a little table in the courtyard and will write your name in swirling letters for a few dirhams.

Madrassa Ben Youssef;
just off Rue Souk el Khemis;
tel: 0524 44 18 93; daily
9am-6pm; charge (combined
tickets including the Musée
de Marrakech, Koubba and
Madrassa are available);
map F2

Break out of your comfort zone and **have lunch** at Marrakech's alternative **food stalls**

Eating at a food stall or grabbing a quick bite from a street vendor may not be everyone's cup of tea, but for die-hard foodies and those who want to try the kind of food that locals eat, it shouldn't be missed. The food stalls of the Jemaa el Fna (*p.35*) are the obvious ones, but why not be a little more adventurous and – in between museum and madrassa-hopping – stop at the little cluster of stalls around the **Place Ben Youssef** (map E1), just outside the **Musée de Marrakech** (*p.86*).

If you're here at breakfast time, try eggs *khli* (eggs with strips of mutton preserved in fat – surprisingly delicious) or *sfinge* (sugary deep fried doughnuts). At lunchtime, choose anything from snail soup, brochettes (kebabs), fried fish, miniature tagines, eggs scrambled with chili and onions, hearty harira soup (lentil, chick pea and tomato) or go for the most simple and filling option – boiled eggs or potatoes dipped in cumin and salt and squashed inside a hot wedge of *khobz* (bread).

For all of this and a drink, you'll pay only a few dirhams and while you eat you'll either be charmed by the hectic stallholder or mesmerized by the goings-on around you: this is the heart of the medina, where motorbikes vie with donkeys for space, vendors call out their wares and goatskins are laid out to dry opposite the Koubba. If you've fallen in love with this style of eating, head to **Chez Bejgéuni** in Guéliz (*p.121*) for dinner.

Hire a bicycle and take a **wild ride** through this fascinating part of the medina

It may seem crazy, but biking round the medina is one of the most exhilarating things to do in Marrakech, and the northern neighbourhood, a quiet residential quarter suffused with history and traditional life, is a fantastic place to do it.

Riding through the twisting *derbs* (alleys) of the medina, smells and sounds will assail you at every turn and speed gives it all a zingy edge. The best time is early in the morning before the crowds, or at dusk . Enter the medina through the historic gate of **Bab Doukkala** and pedal your way through Rue Bab Doukkala, lined with fruit and vegetable stalls, butchers' stalls and tailors. Continue on to the **Rue Dar el Bacha** *(p.91)*, past the **Koubba el Baroudiyn** *(p.101)*, the busy fondouk (merchants' workshops; p.96), the **Chroub ou Chouf Fountain** *(p.100)* and up to Rue de Bab Taghzout, a traditional street of tradesmen and food vendors. At the end of this is an archway that used to mark the northernmost exit of the medina, until it was expanded in the 17th century. Cycle through here and you'll hit the spiritual heart of the city, **Zaouia Sidi Bel Abbès** *(p.95)*. Continue past the mosque and

Berber market outside and wind your way north, to the flea market of **Souk el Khemis** *(p.93)*.

Bikes can be rented by the hour, half-day or day. A half day is between 60–100dh. Good quality bikes can be rented on Place de la Liberté opposite the petrol station and from Maroc Deux Roues.

Maroc Deux Roues, Avenue Mohammed V (opposite Bab Nkob); tel: 0661 59 27 14; map p.105 F2

Take tea in the **sunlit courtyard** of the **Musée de Marrakech**

The superb **Musée de Marrakech**, situated in the restored 19th-century Mnebhi Palace, was the home of Mehdi Mnebhi, chief advisor to Sultan Abdelaziz (1894–1908), and later of Thami el Glaoui. Today, the museum displays a wonderful collection of ethnographic and archaeological objects; Jewish items, including a Torah, oil lamps and a menorah; Islamic calligraphy and a collection of 18th and 19th century lithographs and watercolours of Moroccan ports.

The museum has also built up a fantastic collection of contemporary Moroccan art and regularly holds exhibitions and other cultural events in the central courtyard, the beautiful old hammam and what used to be the kitchens. To top it all off, there is a bookshop selling gorgeous (though expensive) coffee table books on Morocco. Once you have absorbed enough art, culture and architecture, settle down in the lovely sunlit courtyard café with a pot of sweet mint tea and some Moroccan pâtisseries and let it all sink in.

Musée de Marrakech; Place Ben Youssef; tel: 0524 44 18 93; www. museedemarrakech.ma; daily 9am–6pm; charge; map F1

MINT TEA RITUAL

Mint tea – 'Moroccan whisky', as you will often be told – is the national drink par excellence. You will be offered it when you arrive in your hotel, at the end of every meal and in most shops or stalls you visit. Preparing proper mint tea is a long and ceremonial process, with the intention of extracting maximum flavour. Pouring tea from a height cools the liquid and creates the 'ras' or head of froth – a sign of good hospitality.

Marvel at images of old Marrakech at the
Maison de la Photographie

For 15 years, Patrich Manac'h has collected photographs illustrating the history of Morocco. In an extraordinary private initiative, he has chosen to exhibit 5,000 works from his collection at the **Maison de la Photographie**, which opened its doors in 2009.

The photographs, dating from the 1870s to the 1950s, are jaw-droppingly beautiful testaments to a time that has long since disappeared. The first floor contains the work of two Scottish photographers and travellers and focuses on architecture, street scenes and portraits. The second floor has a collection of original plates by René Bertrand, who lived in Guéliz in the 1930s and took portraits of the Berber tribes of the High Atlas. There are also interesting images of the Chellah in Rabat, traditional pisé architecture, the Gnaoua (and even a few by a Moroccan princess, no less). The third floor screens the work of Daniel Chicault, who filmed the first colour documentary on the Berbers. Postcards, posters and books can be bought by the entrance.

Climb a little higher and you will emerge onto one of the loveliest roof terraces in the medina. The red walls are blanketed with bougainvillea, the views are stupendous and there is a delicious menu that includes salads, tagines, sandwiches and lots of mint tea. You'll never want to leave.

Manac'h also runs the **EcoMusée Berbère** in the Ourika Valley *(p.147)*.

Maison de la Photographie; 46 Rue Souk Ahl Fes (follow the signs from the Madrassa Ben Youssef); tel: 0524 38 57 21; www.maisondelaphotographie.ma; daily 9.30am–7pm; charge; map F2

Learn how to **cook a tagine** like a true Moroccan at **La Maison Arabe**

For anyone who loves Moroccan food and wishes they could re-create it at home, a cookery class is a must. It may seem simple, but Moroccan cuisine is refined and elaborate and there is no substitute for a lesson in Morocco itself, taught by a traditional cook.

Classes are mushrooming all over Marrakech but the place that started the whole trend is **La Maison Arabe**. It began with a restaurant that became a bit of a legend. In the 1940s two French women decided to set up the first Moroccan restaurant in the medina, which quickly became not only the best in town but one of the most popular places to hang out (Winston Churchill and the Queen of Denmark were regulars).

Today, the cookery classes, for both amateurs and professionals, are taught by a *dada* (traditional Moroccan cook) or by a chef from the restaurant. Groups range from two to 10 people with private workshops available and there is a translator on hand. At the end of the class – at which you will prepare either a starter and main course or main course and dessert – you can enjoy your creations. Classes start at 600dh per person.

Dar Attajmil (in Central Medina, p.162) is infused with a little bit of Italy, but its half-day cookery course is 100 percent Morocco. At the vibrant food market of Bab Doukkala you will first learn about the best ingredients and spices for a Moroccan feast and stock up on fresh seasonal fruit and vegetables. Back at the riad, you will prepare a starter, main course, dessert, make freshly baked bread and then get to eat everything on the roof terrace or in the cosy sitting room. The only downside (or not, depending on how you look at it) is that you have to be a guest of the hotel to take part.

At **Les Jardins de la Medina** (in Southern Medina, p.158), chef Sanaa will take you on a discovery of the intricacies of Moroccan cuisine. Lessons – which are taken on one of the hotel's terraces with views across the city – can be in a group or solo and are tailored to meet individual requirements and budgets. There is the standard cookery course, at which you bake fresh bread, prepare different Moroccan salads, an elaborate tagine and Moroccan pâtisserie, as well as learning the ritual of mint tea-making. Lunch with wine is included in the 750dh price.

At the 'culinary demonstration', you can learn how to make a typical Moroccan speciality: *pastilla* (450dh), couscous or tagine (390dh) and there is also a 'culinary holiday', where every facet of Moroccan cuisine is explored and foodie excursions offered, for a set price, including accommodation over four days.

La Maison Arabe; 1 Derb Assehbé, Bab Doukkala; tel: 0524 38 70 10; www.lamaisonarabe.com; map B1
Dar Attajmil; 23 Rue el Ksour; tel: 0524 42 69 66; www.darattajmil. com; map p.30, D3
Les Jardins de la Medina; 21 Derb Chtouka; tel: 0524 38 18 51; www. lesjardinsdelamedina.com; map p.56, C3

Have a real-life **Arabian Night** at a romantic **riad restaurant**

Marrakech is one of the most romantic cities in the world and dinner in a riad restaurant is a dreamy experience. When it comes to places that are straight out of *A Thousand and One Nights*, you are spoilt for choice.

Dar Yacout *(pictured)*, in one of the most enchanting riads in the medina, is where royalty and movie stars hang out. Candle-filled lanterns illuminate private salons with fireplaces and hidden corners with carved cedar ceilings. Cocktails are served on the roof and the deliciously extravagant food is eaten around the courtyard pool or an opulent dining room.

Through a labyrinth-like warren, you'll find **Dar Zellij** in a stunning 17th century riad. Tables strewn with rose petals are arranged around a marble fountain. Feast on crispy *briouats*, fish pastilla, lamb tagine with figs or a Marrakchi *tanjia* (slow-roasted lamb). They have just started doing brunch and also offer vegetarian and taster menus.

At **Le Pavillon**, as you are led down a carpeted alley by a man carrying a lantern, you realize you are in for a treat. This is considered the best French restaurant in town. Tables are set under old orange trees, the whitewashed courtyard is stunning in its simplicity and there are cosy alcoves hung with carpets. The food is exceptional: terrine de fois gras, duck breast with apples and herb-encrusted lamb.

All three restaurants serve three course meals for around 1,000dh for two.

Dar Yacout; 79 Derb Sidi Ahmed Soussi, Bab Doukkala; tel: 0524 38 29 29; www.yacout.net; Tue–Sun D; C3
Dar Zellij; Kaasour Sidi Ben Slimane; tel: 0524 38 26 27; www.darzellij.com; daily Br, D; D3
Le Pavillon; 47 Derb Zaouia; tel: 0524 38 70 40; Wed–Mon D; C1

Try not to bankrupt yourself on **Rue Dar el Bacha**

Marrakech is full of surprises when it comes to shopping, and the upscale **Rue Dar el Bacha** (map D2) is one of them. This pretty street curves around the sumptuous **Dar el Bacha** or Dar el Glaoui, Pasha Glaoui's old palace that is now used for the king's guests (closed to the public). This is where the international jet set shops, but even if your wallet doesn't extend to the sky-high prices of the boutiques here, it's still fun to browse.

Zimroda (no.28) is bursting with an amazing collection of antiques, curiosities, jewellery and pottery. The **Khalid Art Gallery** (no.14) is one of the most respected antique shops in town. There are inlaid ivory chests, silver perfume bottles, Moroccan art, ceramics from the Sahara, textiles and French antiques. Rumour has it that the king himself shops here.

The **Librarie Dar el Bacha** (no.2) stocks beautiful tomes on Moroccan art, literature and food (mainly in French). There is also a wonderful collection of old stamps and photographs of Marrakech.

Back towards the palace is the exquisite **Dar Donab** (map D1, see also p.159), a hotel in a

building which used to be part of the palace. It's a lovely place to stop for tea or a spot of lunch and a dip in their pool. This is about as exclusive as it gets (there are only six suites) but the staff are charming and more than happy to accommodate non-guests.

Further along the street, as you get closer to the souks, there are a number of fantastic old fondouks (workshops where you can see craftsmen at work) which are considerably cheaper and worth exploring.

Discover a **treasure trove** of old artefacts in an **Aladdin's cave**

every design – he has six workshops in the medina restoring antiques and creating new pieces. Everything works just as well in New York or Paris as it does in a Marrakech riad, and of course the exoticism adds kudos. As a result, Blaoui's book of contacts includes everyone from Oliver Stone to Ridley Scott and the Clintons to Catherine Deneuve.

Come here to buy translucent alabaster vases, rare Uzbek *suzanis* (elaborately embroidered textiles used for decoration), black and white camel-bone mirrors, kilim-covered armchairs, stretched goatskin Fortuny-style lanterns, woven leather chairs and bed heads, wicker mats from Mauritania... But be warned – don't try to haggle. As Blaoui says, 'This isn't the souk!'

Another repository of stylish goodies nearby is **La Maison de l'Artisanat**, which sells accessories, lanterns and stylish contemporary furniture. Great for gifts or decking out your house.

Behind a heavy wooden studded door, with just the street number as its sign, is a veritable Aladdin's cave of treasures. If you ever wondered where the beautiful lantern, bolt of vintage fabric or Damascene chest of drawers that adorn your riad came from, the answer is probably **Mustapha Blaoui's** *Trésor de Nomades*.

This is where riad owners, movie set designers, stylists, interior designers and travellers-in-the-know come to buy the most exquisite things you will find anywhere in Morocco. So popular is it that Blaoui has had to extend his emporium so there is now double the shopping experience.

Mustapha Blaoui hand picks every piece and commissions

Mustapha Blaoui; 142-144 Rue Bab Doukkala; tel: 0524 38 52 40; email: tresordesmondes@hotmail.com; C2 La Maison de l'Artisanat; 70 Bab Taghzout; tel: 0661 24 25 86; E3

Let your inner **vintage junkie** go wild in Marrakech's colourful **flea market**

Marrakech's main souks, north of Jemaa el Fna, are known to everyone, but the city's flea market, which has a fabulously rich seam of vintage treasures spanning a century, as well as some of the city's most interesting craft workshops, is a relatively undiscovered gem.

Souk el Khemis (Thursday market; map E5) is located at the northeastern corner of the medina and stretches from Bab el Khemis to the northernmost tip. The best entry is at this point. There is just one main artery, running north to south, with smaller alleys leading off it. The main thoroughfare begins with uninteresting everyday items; off to the side, however, are fragrant carpenters' alleys which are fascinating to explore. Here you will find the wonderful reclaimed riad doors and windows (increasingly rare, and expensive) that have become the height of decorative fashion.

Further into the souk (check out the side alleys, off the main drag), come the shops that vintage-lovers will adore. Here you will find everything from Victorian prams, 19th century oil paintings and gramophones to 1960s plastic Panton chairs, retro '70s lighting, Art Deco furniture, African masks, carved Tuareg tent pegs, cast iron baths and a scattering of Moroccan art. At the end of the souk are pottery and wicker workshops and a whole emporium selling bowls, plates and tagine pots, which are much cheaper than in the main souks.

The souk is open every day except Fridays. Thursday is the main market day but also the busiest. Sunday mornings are slightly more peaceful.

Have your very own **kaftan tailor-made**

There is buying a kaftan ready-made from a boutique and there is having one custom-made to your own personal style and specifications. Marrakech is a city where most locals have their clothes made from scratch, which means that the tailors – an old guild in this city of craftsmen – are exceptionally good and also affordable. For 300dh you can have a linen shirt or simple cotton *jellaba* made; for 1,000dh, a pair of tailored trousers or a more elaborate kaftan. Most tailors will be able to finish a piece in 2–5 days. In terms of what to have made, there is a wealth of choice: the iconic kaftan (in a multitude of

styles), the *jellaba* robe (for both men and women, summer and winter), *burnous* (short hooded jellabas for men), linen tunics, embroidered shirts... The best part? Walking away with a one-off piece that you know won't be found anywhere else in the world.

As well as **Beldi** (p.42) and **Aya's** (p.59), there are a couple of excellent tailors opposite Mustapha Blaoui (p.92), who produce chic, elegant linen tunics and kaftans as well as more elaborate pieces. They have swatches of fabric for you to choose from, but if you want more of a selection, go to the large covered clothing market in the Mellah where you can buy by the metre. **Bouriad Karim** is slightly more expensive, but has a fashionable selection of clothes (linen dresses, sparkly kaftans, embroidered jackets) and will tailor-make anything you want.

Marrakech being a city of artisans, it is worth bearing in mind that it's not just clothes that can be custom made. Lanterns, furniture, mirrors – if you have an idea and a little bit of time, anything can be made for you.

Bouriad Karim; Rue Fatima Zohra; tel: 0524 38 65 17; map C1

Walk through the courtyard of **Zaouia Sidi Bel Abbes**, Marrakech's patron saint

Marrakech is protected by seven Sufi saints that serve as spiritual guardians of the city. In the 18th century, a *ziara* pilgrimage was instigated whereby pilgrims would visit the tombs of each saint on a specific day of the week. Of these seven saints, **Sidi Bel Abbes** (1130–1205), patron saint of the city, is the most revered. He devoted his life to the less fortunate, and his shrine – the **Zaouia Sidi Bel Abbes** (map D4) – is a symbol of spiritual Morocco, its magic permeating every

corner of this authentic quarter. The complex houses an abattoir, mosque, cemetery, madrassa and refuge for the blind. Although you can't enter the mosque or shrine, you can walk through the courtyard. Steal a glimpse of the beautiful carved stucco entranceway, the finely painted exterior walls and the magnificent pyramidal tiled roof. This is about as close as you'll get to the beauty of a Moroccan mosque.

Walking through the courtyard from the Bab Taghzout side – passing an old arcade of jewellers, tailors and butchers – you will emerge at the riad of legendary designer, **Bill Willis**, who first arrived in the '60s with Paul Getty Jr and stayed until his death in 2010. Chances are that every design detail in the riad in which you are staying was influenced by him.

GUARDIAN SAINTS
The idea of seven saints – es-Sebti – is ancient. It was Sultan Moulay Ismail who brought the tradition into the mainstream. If you take the Tour des Ramparts *(p.36)* you will notice seven large stone towers near Bab Doukkala. These are locally known as the 'seven men' and refer to the seven guardian saints of the city.

Stroll down Rue Souk Ahl Fes and explore the busy **artisanal life** of a **fondouk**

The fondouks – or merchants' workshops – of Marrakech are living connections to the old trading and artisanal spirit of the city and are intriguing places to visit. The **Rues Souk Ahl Fes** and **Amesfah** and the streets around Dar el Bacha still have functioning fondouks that are as captivating architecturally as they are for what goes on inside. These large riads, centred around a courtyard and decorated surprisingly beautifully, served either as resting places for travellers and merchants who came from across North Africa to trade in Marrakech, or as warehouses and workshops. In the central courtyards, auctions would be held and the little rooms edging the courtyard served as workshops and storerooms.

Visiting a fondouk opens a fascinating window onto old Marrakech, but it's also a great shopping opportunity. Because there is no middleman here and you deal directly with the artisan, you can expect to pay much less than you would in the souks. And buying a piece that has been handmade in front of you makes it that little bit more special.

Look for Moroccan lanterns of every shape and size, carpets, furniture, art and pottery. If you are in Mouassine in the southern medina, check out the fondouk that featured in the film, *Hideous Kinky*, starring Kate Winslet. While you're in the mood, why not have dinner in a fondouk at one of the loveliest restaurants in town – **Le Fondouk**.

Le Fondouk; 55 Souk el Fassi; Kaat Bennahid; tel: 0524 37 81 90; daily L, D; map F2

Explore **Morocco's living culture** at Riad Denise Masson, the Musée de l'Art de Vivre and Dar Bellarj

Marrakech is a magnet for extraordinary people and Denise Masson was one of them. The 'Dame of Marrakech' lived in the city for 60 years. Through her understanding of Arab culture, she was a remarkable example of the positive side of the Franco-Moroccan relationship. On her death, she bequeathed her house to the **Institut Français** *(p.119)* and it has been transformed into the **Riad Denise Masson**, a cultural gathering place that is all about building bridges between east and west.

Listen to traditional musicians or a talk on Arab aesthetics in the courtyard; wander through rooms hung with an exhibition of rare early 20th century photographs of Morocco or the latest paintings from a young local artist.

The **Musée de l'Art de Vivre**, just round the corner, is all about the living culture of Morocco. The ethos of this lovely museum is to provide the traveller with an insight into the heart of Morocco through its art and crafts. At the same time, visitors can discover the art of traditional living in a beautifully restored 19th century riad. For more living heritage, check out **Dar Bellarj** *(pictured)*, the 'Stork's House', another fascinating venue which hosts exhibitions, workshops and other cultural events.

Riad Denise Masson; 49 Derb Zemrane; tel: 0524 44 69 30; Mon–Fri 9am–6pm; map D2
Musée de l'Art de Vivre; 2 Derb Cherif, Diour Saboun; tel: 0524 37 83 73; www.museemedina.com; daily, winter 9am–5pm, summer 9am–6pm; map E2
Dar Bellarj; 9 Rue Toulat Zaouiat Lahdar; tel: 0524 44 45 55; daily 9am–6pm; map E2

Brave a traditional Marrakech **hammam**

The art of the hammam (steam bath/bathhouse) is an ancient and integral part of Moroccan life as water, which is considered sacred, and cleanliness, are essential elements of Islam. In a part of the world where family and community are everything, the hammam is deeply rooted in everyday communal life. This is where people go to socialise, gossip, make connections, do business and even arrange marriages. There are hammams throughout the medina; some are basic – a couple of small tiled rooms, announced by a faded 'Sunsilk' sign – and others are hundreds of years old and full of character, with great domed rooms heated by wood fires under the buildings and multi-coloured

beams of sunlight filtering through stained glass into the steamy darkness within.

Spas with 'traditional' hammams are everywhere in Marrakech, but a visit to a local hammam is a completely different experience and one that illuminates a side of life you won't see anywhere else. This is particularly so for women. For many, especially those who wear the veil, it is one of the only places where they can truly be themselves.

Entry to a local hammam (strictly segregated) is around 10dh. Leave your things in the changing room and take toiletries into the first 'warm' room. This is where you acclimatise to the heat and can collect buckets to fill with water – one cold and one hot. Once accustomed to the heat, move into the second 'hot' room to let your pores open and breathe. Move back to the warm room for your cleanse. This is where you coat yourself in oily black *savon noir* (traditional, 100 percent natural soap made from olive oil) and then use your hammam glove to scrape it – and several layers of your skin – off. Purifying g*hassoul* clay masks can also be smothered all over your body at this stage. In

most hammams, you can have a massage and a *gommage* (scrub) done for you by an attendant for a few extra dirhams. If it all gets too much, just say 'shwiya afak' (gently, please). At the end of it all, you'll look like and feel as good as a shiny newborn baby.

Of all the local hammams in the medina, the **Hammam Dar el Bacha** is one of the most atmospheric. Built in the 1930s by Pasha Glaoui, the entrance has a beautiful dome and the internal rooms are paved in Carrara marble and decorated with fine *zellige* tilework and carved cedar. If a local hammam sounds like too much, there are super luxurious spa hammams that cater solely for tourists. **Beldi** (*pictured; p.128*) and **Ksar Char-Bagh** (*p.131*) are two of the most fabulous.

Hammam Dar el Bacha; 20 Rue Fatima Zohra; women: noon-7pm, men: 7.30pm-midnight; map C1

Watch the world go by at the stunning
Chroub ou Chouf Fountain

In a desert city like Marrakech, water is a precious resource. Amazingly, in spite of this, there are public fountains in every part of the medina, where inhabitants come to replenish their drinking supplies, wash clothes, utensils, even themselves, or just pass the time. Marrakech is threaded by a network of underground water systems and channels that provide for these fountains as well as for mosques and homes.

Wander around the medina and you will spot fountains of all shapes and sizes, from humble brass taps in the walls of streets to something altogether more majestic, like the **Chroub ou Chouf Fountain**.

Built in the 16th century during the reign of Ahmed el Mansour, the fountain is one of the most beautiful examples of how important water is to the city. As grand as a palace, an intricately-carved honeycombed cedar arch drips over the fountain, which is crowned with shining green tiles.

An inscription invites passers by to 'chroub ou chouf' – drink and look. Most people now come to this Unesco World Heritage Site to look at it, rather than drink from it, although it is still very much a working fountain. Stop awhile and follow the ebb and flow of the daily hustle and bustle, buzz and clamour of this ever-changing city. Have lunch nearby at the charming **Souk Kafe** (spot it by the giant teapot balancing on its roof) which has fresh, delicious food at decent prices. If you are in the central medina, check out the lovely **Mouassine Fountain** – another great homage to the importance of water in Marrakech.

Souk Kafe; 11 Derb Souk Jeldid, Sidi Abdelaziz; daily L; map E2

Discover the **Koubba Baroudiyn**, Marrakech's oldest building

Next to the Musée de Marrakech is an (at first glance) unassuming structure that is easily overlooked. But it is arguably one of the most significant buildings in Marrakech. The **Koubba** is the oldest structure in this ancient city and the only surviving example of Almoravid Marrakech.

The Berber Almoravid dynasty (1060–1147) forged an empire that at its height stretched from Mali and Mauritania into southern Spain and Portugal. In 1062 they founded Marrakech and made it the glittering capital of what was one of the most powerful empires in the world. Unfortunately, nothing – except the Koubba – now remains from their time, because the Almohads (1147–1269) destroyed everything when they conquered the city.

An inscription above the entrance to the Koubba states that, 'I was created for science and prayer by the prince of believers…'. Originally built in around 1117, renovated in the 16th and 18th centuries and then buried beneath a newer building, until it was rediscovered in 1948, the Koubba was once part of a larger bathing complex attached to a long lost mosque. This is where the faithful would come to perform their important ablutions before prayers.

The elegant yet stunningly elaborate detail of the dome's interior is truly breathtaking. Stand beneath it and watch the light play across marble that seems to glow from within. You can truly sense Marrakech's rich and ancient past here and, in this city of sand and heat, you are reminded once again of the great significance of water.

Koubba el Baroudiyn; daily, May–Sep 9am-7pm, Oct-April 9am-6pm; combined tickets including the Musée de Marrakech, Koubba and Madrassa are available at the Musée and the Madrassa; map E1

Guéliz

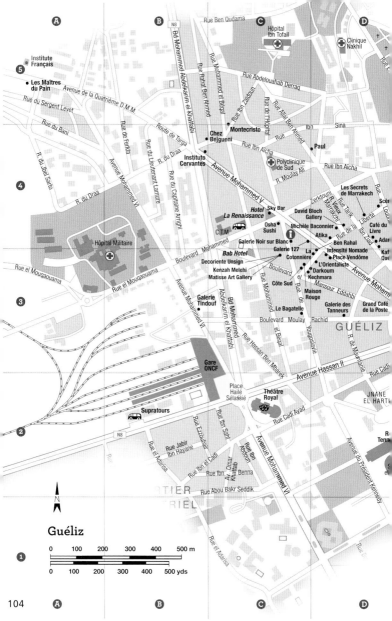

Guéliz

| 0 | 100 | 200 | 300 | 400 | 500 m |

| 0 | 100 | 200 | 300 | 400 | 500 yds |

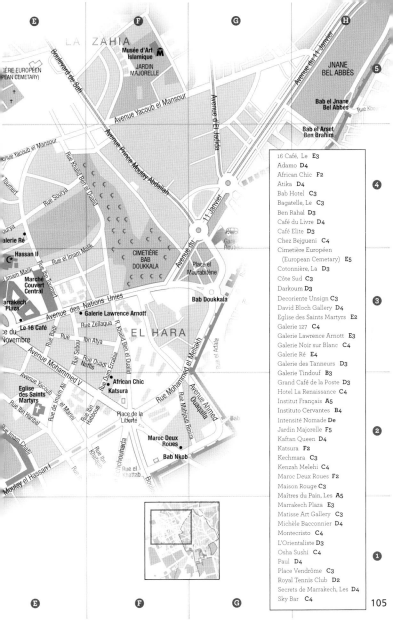

Wander through the delightful **green and shady Jardin Majorelle**

The French painter, Jacques Majorelle, lived in Marrakech for over 40 years. His art is largely forgotten but the gardens that he designed are famous throughout the world. As well as giving his name to the **Jardin Majorelle**, he also gave it to a particular shade of cobalt blue, 'Majorelle blue', which adorns the 1930s Moorish pavilion in the heart of the garden.

Jacques Majorelle died in 1962 and, in 1980, Yves Saint Laurent and his partner, Pierre Bergé, bought the gardens and restored them to their former glory. For both Majorelle and Yves Saint Laurent, the garden was, and remains, a blissfully tranquil place of inspiration and contemplation in the heart of the city.

There are plants from all five continents here; horticulturalists will be in paradise. Wander through the magnificent forest of South Asian bamboo – so unexpected – and along curved pathways dotted with bright turquoise and cobalt pots overflowing with geraniums and succulents. There is a cactus garden full of rare specimens from across the world, dozens of different types of palm, from California to the Canaries; and basins, fountains and ponds full

> ### YVES SAINT LAURENT
> Yves Saint Laurent's passion for Morocco, which spanned over 20 years, is evident in some of his most beautiful clothes that reflect the rich colours, eclectic influences and vibrant culture of the country. Reworking the traditional jellaba, kaftan and *burnous* (long cloak) into chic, flowing, sculptural works of art, YSL managed to encapsulate in fashion what enchanted him about his adopted country.

of aquatic plants worthy of a Monet painting. Alongside the rush and tinkle of water is the sound of 15 different species of birds which live in the trees. And in a shady corner of the garden is a new addition: the stone memorial to Yves Saint Laurent, who died in 2008 and whose ashes were scattered here, in the place he loved above all others.

Having explored outside, step inside the blue pavilion, which houses Saint Laurent's and Bergé's magnificent **collection of Islamic art** (the Musée d'Art Islamique) – ceramics, weapons, jewellery, textiles, carpets and woodwork – from the Maghreb, Africa and Asia, as well as the art of Jacques Majorelle and some riveting photographs of Saint Laurent's glamorous life in

Morocco in the 1970s, '80s and '90s. There are also temporary exhibitions here, the latest being a fabulous retrospective of Saint Laurent's Moroccan-inspired fashion and an exhibition of his iconic New Year's 'love' cards.

The pretty bougainvillea-covered courtyard café is a gorgeous place to stop for tea or a good lunch, and don't forget to peek inside the expensive but rather wonderful boutique shop which has a selection of chic clothing, postcards, coffee table books and other Majorelle-oriented trinkets.

Just outside the gardens, a little cluster of stylish cafés and shops is blossoming: **Kaowa**, a funky juice bar; **La Galerie**, a modern art gallery; **Heritage Berber**, clothes and accessories and **Darat**, a bookshop and gallery.

Jardin Majorelle; Rue Yves Saint Laurent, off Avenue Yacoub el Mansour; tel: 0524 31 30 47; www.jardinmajorelle.com; daily 1 Oct-30 Apr 8am-5.30pm, 1 May-30 Sept 8am-6pm; charge; map F5

Spend an afternoon **browsing the boutiques**
for original gifts and glamorous fashion

If you've had an overdose of exoticism in the medina, head for the Ville Nouvelle, whose streets are lined with tempting shops...

For interiors, **Ben Rahal** (28 Rue de la Liberté, map D3) is where those in the know come to buy carpets. It's a much less hectic experience than the souks and the knowledgeable owner has a fine selection. **Darkoum** (5 Rue de la Liberté, map D3) is a wonderland of antique furniture, art and textiles sourced from India, Africa and Southeast Asia. For gifts, go to **Côté Sud** (4 Rue de la Liberté, map C3): hand painted Moroccan tea glasses, embroidered tablecloths, candles and picture frames. Next door is **Maison Rouge** (6 Rue de la Liberté), the sister shop, selling metallic wallets, perfumes and jewellery. **L'Orientaliste** (11–15 Rue de la Liberté, map D3) has a quirky mix of handmade perfumes and oils, antiques and glassware, and **Decoriente Unsign** (Passage Ghandouri, Rue de Yougoslavie, map C3) sells lighting and furniture.

Michèle Baconnier (6 Rue Vieux Marrakchi, map D4) has leather ballet pumps, flowing kaftans, fine gold jewellery and bags to die for. **Kaftan Queen** (44 Rue Tarik Ibn Ziad, map D4) has elegant kaftans, tunics and clothes for children. **Intensité Nomade**'s (139 Ave Mohammed V, map D3) glamorous Moroccan fashion is at the other end of the scale; **Atika** (map D4) has the best leather shoes and **La Cotonnière** (18 Rue de la Liberté, map D3) sells breezy cotton clothes.

Galerie des Tanneurs (4 Boulevard Moulay Rachid) and **Place Vendôme** (141 Ave Mohammed V, map both D3) have excellent leather and suede bags and jackets.

Eat as if you were in Paris at **La Bagatelle**, a Marrakech institution

The French Protectorate in Morocco, which lasted from 1912 until 1956, had a deep-rooted and long-lasting impact on Moroccan culture. In the early years of the 20th century, Morocco was weak and unstable. Divided by infighting and by the unpopular rule of Alaouite Sultan Abdelhafid, who was considered a puppet of the French, Morocco left itself open to foreign interference. In 1912, the Treaty of Fez brought Morocco under French control and for the next 44 years the fates of both countries were entwined. Today, more French people live in and visit Morocco than any other nationality and Morocco, in turn, has adopted much that is influenced by French culture.

For typically French food, there is really only one place to go. **La Bagatelle**, established in 1949 by the current owner's grandmother, is the oldest French restaurant in Marrakech – a much-loved institution that has seen its fair share of colonial intrigues and expat adventures. This is a place to indulge every nostalgic Francophile whim. The wood panelled walls are a journey back in time: covered in an amazingly evocative collection of black and white photos of the owner's family and of Guéliz, from the early 20th century to the present day. In the tradition of great French brasseries, the food won't disappoint: eggs mimosa, endives with braised ham, duck confit with apples and veal *ravigote*. Eat inside on a winter's day or on the lovely garden terrace, which is cooled by vapour sprays in the summer.

La Bagatelle; 103 Rue de Yougoslavie; tel: 0524 43 02 74; daily L, D; C3

Take in the **fabulous views** with **cocktails on a roof terrace**

If you had preconceptions about Marrakech being solely an old city, you will be in for a surprise on a night out in Guéliz. In the medina, everything shuts down by 10pm, but in the Ville Nouvelle, this is when things start waking up. Trendy kids zip through the streets on bikes and gather in groups to flirt and socialise. Western and Moroccan pop music floats out of bars, cafés and restaurants; the city comes alive. After a day exploring the souks and museums of the medina or shopping in Guéliz, what better way to soak up the balmy, star-

studded Moroccan night than to lounge on a roof terrace with a proper cocktail...

There is absolutely nothing exotic or oriental about the **Bab Hotel**; this is about as urban as it gets. All is chic white minimalism punctured by seriously fashionable art (lately there was an exhibition of Yves Saint Laurent 'Love' postcards) and populated by a hip crowd of Marrakchis and expats. The barman mixes arguably the best Martini in town, the music is suitably chilled and the fabulous Ibiza-style roof terrace is dreamy.

The achingly stylish **Sky Bar** (*pictured*), on the roof of long-time Marrakech institution, **La Renaissance Hotel**, has the best views in town. Lounge on a sofa opposite a vertiginous plunge pool and gaze over the lights of Marrakech, which abruptly and romantically end in a black expanse of desert plain.

Bab Hotel; Corner of Boulevard el Mansour Eddahbi and Rue Mohammed el Beqal; tel: 0524 43 52 50; daily L, D; map C3
Sky Bar, Hotel La Renaissance; 89 corner of Boulevard Mohammed Zerktouni and Mohammed V; tel 0524 33 77 77; daily B, L, D; C4

Enjoy **brunch** in the colonial charm of
Grand Café de la Poste

When you want a more familiar, European-style experience, head for Guéliz. The heart of the Ville Nouvelle revolves around the gleaming new 'Marrakech Plaza', which is lined with European shops, and open-air cafés and restaurants, including **Le 16 Café** *(p.120)*. Just north of the Plaza is a huge **Zara** and **Zara Home** and a buzzing café called **Elite**. There is no alcohol served here, but they do a mean breakfast and reasonable pizzas, paninis and salads for lunch.

Across the street from Elite is what feels like the spiritual heart of Guéliz, the ever-popular **Grand Café de la Poste**. As the name suggests, this fantastically characterful restaurant is situated in the old post office and all the original colonial vibe remains: shuttered French windows, faded black and white floor tiles, wooden ceiling fans lazily fanning the leaves of potted palms.

The terrace is where it's at. Grab a table, order brunch (think eggs and bacon, club sandwiches, smoked salmon and omelettes washed down with fresh orange juice or a Bloody Mary) and people watch to your heart's content. Lunch and dinner are just as good and the bar upstairs is the perfect place to have a pre-dinner drink.

Grand Café de la Poste; corner of Boulevard el Mansour Eddahbi and Rue el Imam Malik; tel 0524 43 30 38; www.grandcafedelaposte.com; daily L, D; map D3

Discover a **tranquil gem** in the heart of the city at the **European Cemetery**

Guéliz – the new town built by the French solely for the purposes of their administration during the Protectorate (1912–56) – is full of reminders of the colonial era: restaurants, villas, old hotels... But one of the strongest remnants – and also one of the least-known sites in Marrakech – is the **European Cemetery**, which dates back to 1925. In the heart of this hectic, noisy and busy modern town the cemetery is an oasis of tranquility – and a surprisingly lovely place to wander round, with its whitewashed tombs overgrown with wild flowers and shaded by towering palm trees.

There are no graves of famous people here, just the men and women who decided to live far away from home. A white obelisk is a reminder of the soldiers who died in North Africa fighting to free France during World War II, an episode recounted in the film *Days of Glory* (2006). The epitaphs trace the history of a colonial power come and gone.

From the cemetery, cross town to Marrakech's only Catholic church, built in 1930 and dedicated to six 13th century Franciscan friars who were beheaded for proselytizing (a crime that remains illegal in Morocco to this day). In an unmistakably oriental and Islamic Marrakech, both these places feel intriguingly out of place and are all the more interesting for it.

COLONIAL GUÉLIZ
Very little of French Guéliz has survived the onslaught of modernity and change in Marrakech – many of the old villas have been torn down to make way for apartment blocks. But here and there you will find poignantly beautiful examples of what must have been. The old cinema on Rue de Yougoslavie and a few apartment buildings on Avenue Mohammed V are particularly wonderful, though sadly decayed.

*European Cemetery; Rue Erraouda;
daily April – Sept, 7am-7pm and
Oct–March, 8am-6pm; free; E5
Eglise des Saints Martyrs; Rue de
Imam Ali; free; E2*

Pamper yourself in urban style at
Les Secrets de Marrakech

In Marrakech, there is the traditional spa – oriental in design, exotic and foreign – and there is the flip side: modern, urban spas that are just as relaxing and luxurious, but more low-key and along the lines of western day spas.

There is something refreshingly different about visiting one of these places in the heart of urban Marrakech – an unusual counterbalance to all the spice and splendour. The ease of getting around the Ville Nouvelle helps too – no meandering, nameless streets to negotiate.

After a day's shopping, wander into **Les Secrets de Marrakech** in the heart of Guéliz and enjoy an hour's Balinese, tonifying or reflexology massage where only argan and natural plants are used in the oils; or a rose facial or hydrating manicure and pedicure. The ever-stylish **Bab Hotel** *(p.110)* has an uber-minimalist spa to match the pared-back décor of the hotel, where the pampering is all done with delicious Carlota Paris products, and there is also a small fitness centre. If you are in the Hivernage neighbourhood, splash out at the magnificent **Es Saadi Palace Spa** *(pictured)*, where you can choose from bio herbal baths,

chromatherapy, ice fountains and Finnish-style saunas or Dior face and body treatments.

Les Secrets de Marrakech; 62 Rue de la Liberté; tel: 0524 43 48 48; www.lessecretsdemarrakech.com; map D4 Bab Wellbeing; corner of Boulevard el Mansour Eddahbi and Rue Mohammed el Beqal; tel: 0524 43 52 50; www.babhotelmarrakech.com; map C3 Es Saadi Palace Spa; Rue Ibrahim el Mazini; tel: 0524 44 88 11; www.essaadi.com; map p.125, G1

Spend a morning discovering **Marrakech's best art galleries**

Moroccan art is experiencing a striking renaissance. Today, it's less about neo-orientalist folk art and more about alternative forms of expression and technique being explored by a young, exciting group of artists. Marrakech is at the forefront of this scene and Guéliz is scattered with some superb galleries.

In fact, so vibrant is the contemporary Moroccan art scene that 2010 saw the first ever **Marrakech Art Fair** (*pictured*; www.marrakechartfair.com), which held wonderfully diverse exhibitions, installations and video art by Moroccan and international artists from 30 countries across North Africa, the Middle East and Europe. If you are in Marrakech in the months of September and October, it's worth a visit.

There is also the popular **Arts in Marrakech (AiM) Biennale** (www.marrakechbiennale.org) – a five day event in February/March exhibiting local and international artists with the intention of bridging cultural gaps through visual art, film and literature.

In Guéliz, take a morning to gallery-hop between the best the city has to offer. The **Matisse Art Gallery** (61 Rue de Yougoslavie, No. 43 Passage Ghandouri, map C3) is one of the oldest, and showcases the talents of the next generation. Acclaimed **Galerie Ré** (Residence Al Andalus III, corner of Rues de la Mosquée and Ibn Toumert, map E4) is an incredibly glamorous, unapologetically modern space that mixes painting, sculpture, photography and installations from Morocco, Europe and the Middle East.

Galerie Tindouf (22 Avenue Mohammed VI, map B3) has a stunning collection of rare Fassi ceramics, precious textiles, Indian miniatures, Islamic calligraphy, 19th century French Orientalist painting as well as revolving exhibitions of contemporary painting and photography. Super stylish **Galerie 127** (127 Avenue Mohammed V, 2nd floor; map C4) was the first photography gallery in the Maghreb and the third in Africa when it opened in 2003. Situated in a beautiful 1920s apartment building, the white space with huge French windows places the emphasis on captivating exhibitions by mostly French and Moroccan photographers. It doesn't get more contemporary than the inspiring art at the **David Bloch Gallery** (8 Rue Vieux Marrakchi;

map D4), which celebrates street art in particular (hugely popular in Marrakech – keep an eye out for spontaneous exhibitions in disused spaces) and has positioned itself at the very heart of the contemporary art scene.

Galerie Noir sur Blanc (48 Rue de Yougoslavie, 1st floor; map C4) is a dynamic, interactive space with monthly exhibitions and an array of activities from workshops, readings and book signings to theatre and musical performances. The **Galerie Lawrence Arnott** (Immeuble el Khalil, Ave des Nations Unies; map F3) began life in London in 1975 and is one of the only spaces devoted to more traditional art in Marrakech. Here you will find figurative paintings by both Moroccan and European artists, including Jacques Majorelle and Hamri.

Listen to **live music** on a hot summer night

The 1960s author and painter Brion Gysin thought hearing the music of Morocco was enough to make anyone become a Muslim. The Rolling Stones didn't go quite that far, but they did dress in jellabas to record the track 'Continental Drift' with Moroccan group, Master Musicians of Jajouka, for their 1989 album Steel Wheels. Other ground-breaking bands inspired by the eclectic sounds of Morocco include Led Zeppelin, Jimi Hendrix, Ry Cooder and The Beatles.

Music is at the heart of every night out in Marrakech and live music is particularly popular.

Head to laidback **Kechmara** – a hipster joint with trendy art (all for sale) on the walls, retro 1960s furniture, delicious food including great breakfasts and a cool urban roof terrace. There is live music downstairs every Wednesday, Thursday, Friday and Saturday night, when the place gets packed.

Ignore the name and check out **African Chic**, where on any given night you will come across young Moroccans dancing the salsa or tango with such style and passion you will think you have walked into a bar in Rio. The live band kick starts every evening and is followed by a DJ. The Latin vibe continues at lavish **Montecristo**, which has a 'Bar Latino' and a 'Bar Africain' pumping out live music every night from 10.30. **Jad Mahal, So Bar** (p.126) and **Lotus** in Hivernage also stage live music most nights. It's worth noting that nothing gets going in Marrakech until at least 11pm.

Kechmara; 3 Rue de la Liberté;
tel: 0524 42 25 32; www.kechmara.com;
Mon–Sat B, L, D; map C3
African Chic; 6 Rue Oum Errabia;
tel: 0524 43 14 24; daily; map F2
Montecristo; 20 Rue Ibn Aicha;
tel: 0524 43 90 31; daily; map C5

Lounge about in **literary bliss** at the **Café du Livre**

When a Dutch expat who had been living in Morocco for nearly 20 years couldn't find anywhere decent to go to grab a coffee and a book, she decided to set up her own literary café (the first in Marrakech). The **Café du Livre** became an instant hit with both residents and travellers and has remained a much-loved hang-out and meeting place ever since.

After a day exploring the city, this café is a blissful haven of peace. With the atmosphere of a private club, it is cosily warmed by an open fire in winter and cooled by welcome air conditioning in summer.

Antique Persian textiles (family heirlooms) line the walls, the seating is deliciously comfortable and the library (everything is for sale) is filled with over 2,000 books, fiction and non-fiction, in both English and French. Sink into a deep sofa, grab a book and a drink and while away as many hours as you want. There is free Wi-fi, too, for those who want to catch up with the outside world.

The menu – served all day – was created by Michelin-starred chef Richard Neat and has settled into a great selection of freshly made dishes: Caesar salads, hamburgers (the best in town), hearty soups, oven-baked Camembert, garlic-roasted chicken, freshly baked pâtisseries and full breakfasts (courses range from 40–95dh).

Cocktails are served in the evenings until 9pm and there is also draft beer on tap. What more could you ask for...?

Café du Livre; 44 Rue Tarik Ibn Ziad; tel: 0524 43 21 49; Mon–Sat B, L 9.30am–9pm; map D4

Take a break from tagines and head to an **Asian restaurant for lunch**

After a few days of tagines, couscous and *pastilla*, you may want a change, so spice things up with lunch at an Asian restaurant.

Katsura is one of the best. The Thai chef whips up mouth-watering Thai and Japanese dishes that are of a quality as good as anything you'll find in New York, London – or Thailand, for that matter. There are all the usual favourites such as green and red chicken curries, fresh beef, vegetable and prawn stir fries and fragrant noodle soups. The sushi and sashimi menu has everything from California to crispy king prawn rolls and the set menus for 100dh are excellent value.

Urban **Osha Sushi** is a proper sushi bar – all green and white minimalism; quick, fresh sushi prepared by the Japanese chef and a refined selection of Japanese teas. Expect to pay around 100dh per person. In Hivernage, visit **Mai Thai**, which has a lunch menu for 159dh, but is best in the evening in the beautiful Zen garden. In the Palmeraie, there is **Geisha,** which serves good sushi and tepanyaki. Prices start from 200dh.

Katsura; Rue Oum Errabia; tel: 0524 43 43 58; daily L, D; map F2
Osha Sushi; 43 Rue de Yougoslavie; tel: 0524 42 00 88; daily L, D; map C4
Mai Thai; Villa Saumurois, corner Rue de Paris and Avenue Echouhada; 0524 45 73 01; daily L, D; map p.125, G2
Geisha; Palmeraie Golf Palace, Circuit de la Palmeraie; tel: 0524 36 87 69; daily, L, D; p.124, map C5

Be a culture vulture and check out the
Institut Français or **Instituto Cervantes**

Francophone culture is obviously a strong influence in many aspects of Moroccan history and life. If you want to explore this side of the country, head to the **Institut Français**, Marrakech's leading cultural organisation. The Institut has a vibrant selection of entertainment revolving around the unique literary, artistic, theatrical, musical and intellectual fusion of French and Moroccan culture. On any given week, they will be hosting a theatrical or dance performance; holding a new exhibition of contemporary Moroccan art, sculpture or photography; organising lectures and talks or putting on an evening of dance, ballet or music. Excellent art house films are screened in the Institut's large cinema every Wednesday and there is also an extensive library and French language courses. The director of the Institut was instrumental in establishing the **Riad Denise Masson** (p.97).

From France to Spain, that other significant foreign influence in Morocco, which can be felt mostly in the north of the country and remains prevalent in cities like Tangier and the Spanish enclaves of Ceuta and Melilla.

The **Instituto Cervantes** holds a fascinating range of cultural activities revolving around all things Spanish. Having had your Francophone hit – or if you are just more interested in Spanish culture – head to the Cervantes, where you can see flamenco recitals and Spanish film screenings, lectures on various aspects of Spanish culture and history, art exhibitions, dance and music recitals, and literary readings.

Institut Français; Route de Targa, Jbel Guéliz; tel: 0524 44 69 30; daily 9am-6pm, closed July-Sept; charge; map A5
Instituto Cervantes de Marrakech; 14 Avenue Mohammed V; tel: 0524 42 20 55; daily; charge; map B4

Treat yourself to the **best pâtisserie in town**

Morocco wouldn't be Morocco without its pâtisserie. Of all the things that the French left behind, their pâtisserie is surely the most popular, perhaps due to the Moroccan sweet tooth but also because of the similarity with traditional Moroccan desserts such as *halwa chebbakia* (deep fried pastry dipped in honey and sesame seeds) and *cornes de gazelles* ('gazelle horns' – pastry filled with almond paste).

Le 16 Café is a stylish place where you can sit on the Marrakech Plaza and watch the world go by. There is all the usual café fare (croque monsieurs, paninis and salads) but it's the exquisite pâtisserie that's the real draw: mini fruit tarts, chocolate fondants, millefeuilles, chocolate truffles and honey-soaked baklava. Fill a box to take away with you.

Popular with residents, **Adamo** is pleasantly understated, tucked away next to the **Café du Livre** *(p.117)*. Fresh croissants, bread and cakes are baked every morning, so it's a great place for breakfast. **Les Maîtres du Pain** is a traditional boulangerie and pâtisserie and the place where all the restaurants – and savvy locals – come to stock up on delicious fresh bread. It's a lovely place to stop for a pot of tea and a cake or *viennoiserie*, too. To much excitement, a branch of the boulangerie **Paul** recently opened in Marrakech and its lovely terrace is always packed at breakfast time.

Le 16 Café; 16 Place du 16 Novembre, Marrakech Plaza; daily B, L, D; map E3
Adamo; 44 Rue Tarik Ibn Ziad; daily B, L; map D4
Les Maîtres du Pain; 26 Route de Targa; daily B, L; B5
Paul; Rue Allal Ben Ahmed; daily B, L; map D4

Have dinner one evening with **the locals** at **Chez Bejgueni**

Few Moroccans can afford to eat out at the sort of restaurant westerners are familiar with. They also know that the best food is cooked at home. There are a few exceptions, however, like the food stalls in Jemaa el Fna (*p.35*), the sizzling grills on wheels, and dozens of tiny hole-in-the-wall places serving steaming tagines. Somewhere between these and a more traditional restaurant is **Chez Bejgueni**, a bit of a local legend...

Tucked away down one of the prettiest tree-lined streets in Guéliz, this Marrakech institution is where locals and those in-the-know come to eat. Chez Bejgueni opened in 1973 and is still run today by the founder's son. On a balmy summer's night, there is

no lovelier place to soak up a bit of authentic local atmosphere. Sit at one of the tables outside under the trees – be prepared to share – and order whatever looks good that day (there is no menu).

Specialities not to be missed are the kefta sandwich (made with spicy meatballs) – smother it with lashings of the spicy harissa and fresh tomato sauce that come with everything – brochettes, lamb cutlets and grilled chicken. Salad, seriously good fries and crusty bread come with everything and drinks are soft. The price varies, but expect to pay around 50dh per person for food and drink.

Chez Bejgueni; Rue Ibn Aicha; daily L, D; map C4

Hivernage, Menara, Palmeraie, Environs

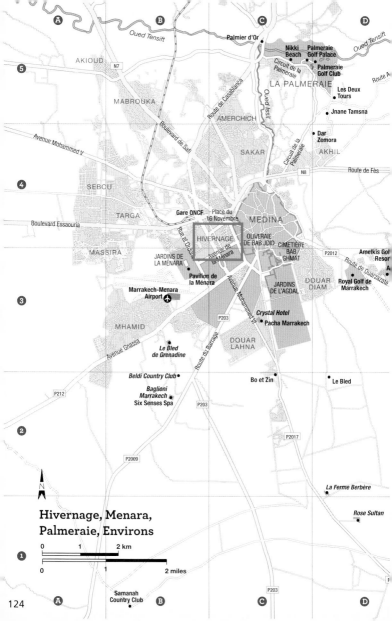

Hivernage, Menara, Palmeraie, Environs

0 1 2 km

0 1 2 miles

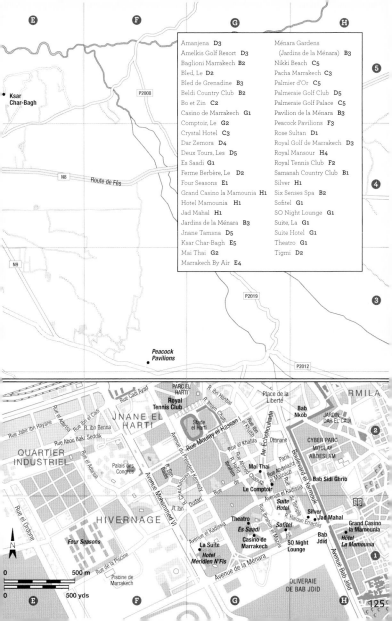

Dance till dawn at one of the city's hottest **nightclubs**

Marrakech: the new Ibiza...? Maybe not, but the city does have some super hip nightclubs and bars that stand up to anything Europe has to offer. Marrakech nights are all about high octane glamour in opulent surroundings, so dress up, hit one of the best venues in town and let your hair down...

Pacha Marrakech (Zone hôtelière d'Agdal, Avenue Mohammed VI; tel: 0524 38 84 00; map C3) is the queen of Marrakchi nightclubs. This legendary club opened in 2005 and includes a decadent nightclub, with DJs including David Guetta and Eric Morillo featuring, and the live-music lounge **Rose Bar**.

For a wilder night, try **Silver** (10 Rue Haroun Errachid; tel: 0524 42 35 37; map H1), where DJs spin techno and house in a state-of-the-art nightclub, or **Theatro** (*pictured*; Rue Ibrahim el Mazini; tel: 0664 86 03 39; map G1), designed like a theatre, with weirdly-costumed performers and a good line-up of Moroccan and international DJs.

Other popular venues are the **SO Night Lounge** (in the Sofitel hotel; Rue Haroun Errachid; tel: 0656 51 50 09; map G1) which stages a mixture of live bands and house music; **La Suite** (Hôtel le Meridien N'Fis; Avenue Mohammed VI; tel: 0524 42 07 00; map G1), a more intimate venue for the jet set crowd, and **Bo et Zin** (Douar Lahna; Route de l'Ourika 3.5km; tel: 0524 38 80 12; map C2), an Asian restaurant in a beautiful garden, which doubles as a classy cocktail hang-out.

Le Comptoir (Rue Ahmed Chaouqi; tel: 0524 43 77 02; map G2) is where you'll see the classiest belly-dancing in town, and **Jad Mahal** (10 Rue Harroun Errachid; tel: 0524 43 69 84; map H1) has live music and extravagant food in fabulously opulent, exotic surroundings.

Watch the sun set over the enchanted Menara Gardens

Some 160km (100 miles) from the coast and far below the cooling Atlas Mountains, Marrakech is a furnace in summer. By two in the afternoon the sun's rays are so fierce that the air itself trembles from the onslaught. For Marrakchis, relief is found in dark interiors, private courtyards and in the city's gardens.

Arguably the most ethereal are the **Menara Gardens and Pavilion**. Created in the 12th century by Almohad sultan, Abd al Mu'min, the gardens are a lovely place to visit, especially between the months of December and April, when the snow-capped Atlas rise up in the distance and are reflected in the rectangular pool that was created as a reservoir (one of the most iconic images of Marrakech). The 16th century pavilion was used by sultans for summertime escapes and romantic liaisons – legends tell of displeased sultans flinging their courtesans into the reservoir – and was restored by Moulay Abderrahman in the 19th century.

Surrounding this tranquil scene are groves of olive and orange trees which, at weekends, are full of strolling Marrakchis. If you're travelling with kids, there are camels and Shetland ponies outside the gates of the Menara, which can be ridden.

A word of caution – package tourists arrive by the coach load at weekends. If you visit first thing in the morning or in the hour just before the gates close, the light is at its most beautiful and you will have the place virtually to yourself.

Menara Gardens; Avenue de la Menara; daily 8.30am–sunset; free; map B3

Leave the hustle behind and spend the day at a **poolside oasis**

Whatever your style, cool off at one of these blissful poolside escapes...

For those who like a bit of glitz and a good people-watch, the fashionable pool of the **Crystal** restaurant at **Pacha** (Zone hôtelière d'Agdal, Avenue Mohammed VI; tel: 0524 38 84 00; map C3) is about as glamorous as it gets. Trendy music and the pop of champagne corks fill the air – this is definitely not a place to read your book quietly – and the food is exceptional.

Nikki Beach (of St Tropez and Miami fame; La Palmeraie; tel: 0663 51 99 92; map C5) is all about seeing and being seen. The lake-like pool, surrounded by white day beds, muscled waiters and thumping dance music contributes to the party atmosphere and the food is also surprisingly good.

If, instead, you want elegance, tranquillity and luxury, head to the magnificent **Les Deux Tours** – a wonderful villa (also a hotel, p.173; Douar Abiad, La Palmeraie; tel: 0524 32 95 27; map D5) that used to be the private home of architect, Charles Boccara. In the heart of the Palmeraie, Les Deux Tours nestles in beautifully lush gardens. Delicious lunches

are served in a breezy poolside pavilion and there is also a spa.

In the same vein, **Beldi Country Club** (also a hotel, *pictured*; p.174; Km6, Route de Barrage; tel: 0524 38 39 50; map B2) is set in acres of scented rose gardens and has one of the most stunning pools in Marrakech – long and thin, between an avenue of 100 year-old olive trees. Three course lunches at a very reasonable set price are laid on by the pool; the spa, with its own herb garden and all-natural

massages, hammams and facial treatments, is not to be missed, and the wonderful pottery and carpet ateliers at the end of the garden are also worth exploring.

For something a little less extravagant, head to **Le Bled de Grenadine** (Km5, Route de l'aéroport; tel: 0661 45 17 90; map B3). This home-from-home is run by the fantastically friendly Grenadine, who cooks Moroccan-Provençal food fresh from her garden. Donkeys, turtles, dogs and cats roam the pretty garden and on clear days you can see the Atlas as you float in the pool. Grenadine also rents lovely

rooms (*p.173*). **Le Bled** (Douar Coucou, Oasis Hassan II; tel: 0524 38 59 39; map D2) is not to be confused with the above, but is similarly charming and refreshingly good value. Lunch usually involves a tagine, a plate of succulent mixed grill and a selection of Moroccan salads, washed down with a bottle of local rosé. The quirky pool is surrounded by a lilac-painted wall and is a peaceful spot to have a siesta after such indulgences.

Reservations at all these places are advised. Charges on top of lunch may apply.

129

Play tennis in the cool of an early morning

If you are a fitness fiend, what could be more exotic than a game of tennis in the shadow of the snow-capped High Atlas? During the winter and spring, temperatures are cool enough to play at any time of day, but in the summer, make sure you head out in the early morning or evening.

Though not technically in this neighbourhood, the oldest – established in 1926 by Hassan II, who loved tennis (and whose photos adorn the walls) – and still arguably the best, is the **Royal Tennis Club** and so must be mentioned here. There are nine clay courts, four of which are floodlit at night, a pool, restaurant, café and spectacular views of the High Atlas. Courts cost 100dh an hour and there are

teachers for those who want one.

Es Saadi has a clay tennis court and the added luxury of a fully-equipped gym, a stylish pool, a spa (*p.113*) and three restaurants, all set in beautifully kept grounds in the heart of the city. The one catch is that only residents of the hotel are allowed access, though it is free. The multi-activity **Palmeraie Golf Palace** has courts that can be used by non-residents (80dh for one hour), as well as football, volleyball and basketball.

Royal Tennis Club; Rue Oued el Makhazine; tel: 0524 43 19 02; daily 7am–noon and 2.30–10.30pm; map G2
Es Saadi; Rue Ibrahim el Mazini; tel: 0524 44 88 11; map G1
Palmeraie Golf Palace; La Palmeraie; tel: 0524 36 87 04; map C5

Pamper yourself at one of the world's most **exclusive spas**

Marrakech's five-star hotels have spas that are the ultimate in glorious self-indulgence.

Ksar Char-Bagh is not only one of the most beautiful places to stay in Marrakech *(p.171)*, with one of the finest restaurants, it has an indescribably lavish hammam. Designed to evoke traditional Turkish steam baths, the dark grey, marble-lined, vaulted octagonal room is lit only by candles and scented with eucalyptus. You will walk out feeling reborn.

With 17 treatment rooms, private pavilions with gardens and a Watsu pool for couples, **Le Spa** at the **Four Seasons** *(pictured)* is everything you would expect from this five star resort. Treatments, inspired by both Middle Eastern and Western traditions, are holistic and organic and incorporate

local plants such as saffron, rose, olive, orange and argan. There are rituals to restore your bio-rhythmns, awakening oxygen facials and bio-energy mud wraps. The **Six Senses Spa** at the **Baglioni Marrakech**, which is scheduled to open in 2013, will incorporate hammams and private relaxation rooms. Guests will be pampered by internationally trained therapists, with a focus on 'Slow Life' – all about natural beauty and total relaxation.

Ksar Char-Bagh; La Palmeraie;
tel: 0524 32 92 44; map E5
Le Spa, Four Seasons; Rue de la Piscine;
tel: 0524 35 92 00; map E1
Six Senses Spa, Baglioni Marrakech;
Km8 Route d'Amizmiz: tel: 0524 39 09
30; due to open in 2012; map B2

Cross your fingers and **roll the dice** one evening at a **casino**

Marrakech has two fabulously glamorous casinos that are fun to spend an evening in, whether gambling or not. Soak up some old-school charm, roll the dice and see where they land.

Established in 1952, the **Casino de Marrakech** was the first to open in Morocco and has become a legendary stop on the gambling circuit, hosting a step on the World Poker Tour as well as national poker championships. Set in the majestic grounds of the Es Saadi (*p.113*), this characterful casino was recently restored to its former glory and boasts 90 slot machines and 24 gaming tables offering blackjack, poker and roulette. In the early days of the casino, stars such as Josephine Baker and Maurice Chevalier used to entertain guests; today, the entertainment takes the form of belly dancers, folk musicians and cover bands. There is also a dining area and Art Deco-style bar, should you need a little fortification.

The other grand old institution of Marrakech casinos is none other than the **Grand Casino La Mamounia** (in Southern Medina). You could be in Vegas in the glitzy gaming room, which has 180 slot machines, 20 traditional table games and a room dedicated to Live Poker, with nightly games. The gourmet restaurant and bar overlooking the gaming room has a weekly wine tasting and a live band.

Casino de Marrakech; Rue Ibrahim el Mazini; tel: 0524 44 88 11; nightly, slots 2pm–4am, gaming tables 8pm–4am, until 5am at weekends; map G1
Grand Casino La Mamounia; Avenue Bab Jdid; tel: 0524 44 45 70; nightly, slots 3pm–6am, gaming tables 9pm–6am; p.56, map A6

Art, literature and inspiration... all at two unique boutique hotels

In a city full of hotels of every style, shape and size, why not stay at one that is a little bit different...? A combination of inspired design and an inspiring philosophy makes **Jnane Tamsna** *(pictured)* a captivating place.

The breathtaking villas, set in a 'lush edible landscape' are inspired by Morocco, Andalusia and Africa. Each feels like a private home and is adorned with antiques and art. There are regular gatherings that provide an insight into this part of the world, such as literary salons (which luminaries like Esther Freud, Barbara Trapido and William Dalrymple have attended) and exhibitions of painting, photography and furniture. When you've had your cultural fill, you can stock up on delicious natural gourmet oils, soaps, preserves and spice mixtures – all created from the gardens.

Just as inspiring is **Peacock Pavilions**, a very special boutique hotel in the heart of an olive grove, which the owner and her architect husband have filled with exquisite objects from their travels around the world, bespoke furniture they have designed, romantic Moroccan tents and vintage textiles, kilims and

carpets (and real live peacocks). As well as being a blissfully tranquil place to get away from it all, Peacock Pavilions holds regular retreats which involve everything from henna and cocktail parties to escorted shopping trips to the souks, wine tastings and creative design workshops.

Jnane Tamsna; Douar Abiad, La Palmeraie; tel: 0524 32 84 84; www. jnanetamsna.com; map D5
Peacock Pavilions; Km13 Route de Ouarzazate; tel: 0524 48 46 17; www. peacockpavilions.com; F3

133

Play a **round of golf** against the **dramatic backdrop** of the High Atlas Mountains

In recent years, Morocco has begun to position itself as one of the foremost golfing destinations in the world, with Marrakech as the jewel in the crown. There are dramatic courses set in palm-fringed oases in the shadow of the High Atlas, which are snow-covered from December to April and a year-round climate that is sunny and warm (though avoid the months of July and August).

The oldest course in Morocco is the **Royal Golf de Marrakech** (18 holes, par 72). Founded by Pasha Glaoui in 1923, Winston Churchill, David Lloyd George and Eisenhower have all played here. Ancient eucalyptus, palm and olive trees edge the course and the High Atlas rise up as the backdrop to most greens. There is a lovely restaurant, too, which is

> **THE KING'S GOLF TROPHY**
> The Hassan II Golf Trophy, named after the current king's grandfather who was passionate about golf and developed the sport in Morocco, is in its 38th year. It is held every spring in Agadir and attracts top ranking international players.

very popular at weekends. Lessons and caddies available.

Created by legendary golf course architect, Robert Trent Jones, the 5 star **Palmeraie Golf Palace** (18 holes, par 72) is another stunning course. Extending over 100 hectares (247 acres), this championship length course has seven beautiful lakes and fantastic views to the High Atlas. Each hole has several tees, adapting to players of all levels. The **Amelkis Golf Resort** (18 holes, par 72)

includes luxury villas with direct access to the greens and is known as one of the most technically challenging courses in Marrakech. The long, rolling fairways are lined with groves of palm trees and stands of giant papyrus.

Like the Amelkis, the **Samanah Country Club** is a five-star 300 hectare (740 acre) resort, with luxury villas all edging the 18 hole, par 72 golf course. The resort offers the David Leadbetter Golf Academy, a driving range with grass teeing area, buggies and caddies, the Golfer's Bar, a restaurant and a kids' club.

Rates for all start at around 500dh per day. For more information, contact the Royal Moroccan Golf Federation, Rabat, tel: 0537 75 56 36.

Royal Golf de Marrakech; Ancienne Route de Ouarzazate; tel: 0524 40 98 28; map D3

Le Palmeraie Golf Palace; La Palmeraie; tel: 0524 36 87 04; map C5

Amelkis; Km12, Route de Ourarzazate; tel: 0524 40 44 14; map D3

Samanah Country Club; Route d'Amizmiz; tel: 0524 84 18 84; map B1

Take a mini **camel safari** around Marrakech's **ancient palm grove**

The date palm was cultivated as far back as 4000 BC and has deep spiritual significance in Morocco, where it is revered as medicinal and nourishing (it is said that a person can survive on one date a day in the desert, with nothing else to sustain them).

The date palm oasis is a source of life, providing food, water and shade, and you are reminded of Marrakech's role as an oasis when you explore the city's Palmeraie. This immense grove has in the region of 190,000 date palms, which were said to have sprung up from the discarded date stones of the Almohad army who besieged the city in the 12th century.

Today, the Palmeraie is home to Marrakech's rich and famous, and palatial villas and hotels set in luxuriant gardens abound. Abandon all thoughts of getting a glimpse into these rarefied worlds, but if you harbour romantic Lawrence of Arabia fantasies and won't have the chance to venture into the desert proper, a camel ride in the palm grove is the next best thing.

The **Palmier d'Or** (p.124, C5) is a decent place for lunch, and most camel rides set off from here. Rides – lasting from half an hour to two hours – meander through the palm groves and on clear days you will catch glimpses of the Atlas. After the manic medina, the steady plodding of these great 'ships of the desert' is surprisingly relaxing (although very bumpy). A stop is usually made for mint tea, but if you are organising this through your riad, you could ask them to make up a picnic for you.

Price: around 100dh for an hour.

See Marrakech from a different perspective on a
hot-air balloon ride

Having explored every inch of Marrakech on foot, by calèche, by bike or by taxi, why not try something different? Take to the air and embark on a hot-air balloon ride over the Red City.

Ciel d'Afrique has been going for 20 years. You are collected from your hotel by experienced pilot and owner, Maurice (who ballooned across the Sahara), before dawn and driven to the flight area. The sight of the giant multi-coloured balloon – one of the largest in the world – slowly inflating (with air that reaches 100° Celsius) against the early morning sky is breathtaking. As the ropes are released and you float up into the blue you are struck by the beauty of it all: the desert plain, tiny olive and orange groves, 'biblical' Berber villages and the majestic High Atlas. On landing, you are taken to a Berber village for mint tea and fresh bread dipped in home-made olive oil. For a little extra, take a VIP flight where you have the balloon to yourself and are served champagne.

Marrakech By Air offers a similar service: collection at dawn and transportation to the flight area, where you are involved in the preparations, followed by a cloud-skimming flight. On landing, you are met by the ground crew who set up a tent with a view of the Atlas and serve a traditional breakfast.

Ciel d'Afrique; Imm. Ali, appt. 4, Avenue Youssef ben Tachfine; tel: 0524 43 28 43; www.cieldafrique.info
Marrakech By Air; 185 Lalla Haya Targa; tel: 0524 49 07 99; www. marrakechbyair.com

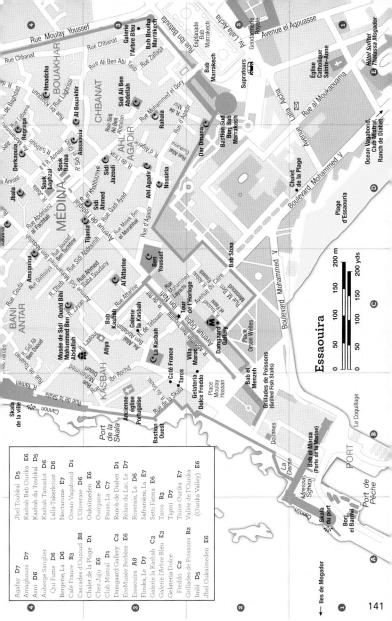

Essaouira

0 50 100 150 200 m
0 50 100 150 200 yds

Head out of the city and explore the **mountains of the High Atlas**

With many of the most beautiful and culturally-interesting places in Morocco being inaccessible by car, trekking and walking are often the best ways to experience what many feel is the true Morocco. In these regions you are rewarded by an unhurried pace, can visit places untouched by the modern world, spend time with local people and see some of the most spectacular scenery in the country.

Just an hour from Marrakech is the monumental High Atlas mountain range (450 miles long with summits over 4,000 metres/13,100ft) and, though most come to trek for several days, a day trip is enough to give a tantalizing snapshot. Life in this sublimely beautiful region has changed very little in centuries, illuminating a side of Morocco

that has largely been forgotten in urban Marrakech and will leave a lasting imprint on all who visit.

The road from Marrakech leads to **Asni**, where there is a Saturday souk with food and livestock, carpets, fossils and other local trinkets. To the south of Asni towers **Jbel Toubkal**, at 4,167 metres (13,700ft) the highest mountain in North Africa. The first recorded ascent of Toubkal was not made until 1923 and testifies to the tribal fortress mentality maintained by local Berbers well into the 20th century. But times have changed since then.

Outside Asni is Richard Branson's super luxe resort, **Kasbah Tamadot**, which is worth a stop for tea or lunch – the views across the gentle foothills all around are lovely. Beyond, in the shadow of Jbel Toubkal, is

the rugged village of **Imlil**. The best place to base yourself for the day is the magical **Kasbah du Toubkal**, which perches above the town and is one of the most stunning hotels in Africa. So beautiful, and with views so reminiscent of the Tibetan Himalayas, that Martin Scorsese filmed his biopic of the Dalai Llama, *Kundun*, here.

Arrive in the morning, have coffee on a terrace with mind-blowing views, then head up into the surrounding foothills. The Kasbah organises walks and day treks that cater to all levels of fitness and last from 45 minutes to seven hours. Mule treks can also be arranged. The stunning walks pass through fruit orchards and take in waterfalls, saints' tombs and mountain villages where you can stop for tea.

Return to the Kasbah for a hearty Moroccan lunch (around 150dh) then escape to the hammam to steam away aches and pains or read a book by the roaring fire. On full day treks a picnic is provided and you can spend the night in a village or back at the Kasbah. The Kasbah also organises day camel excursions, with lunch, about an hour from Marrakech. The best part is that a percentage of the profits is given to the Imlil Village Association, which funds essentials like 4x4 ambulances, schools and clinics.

Unless you are an experienced hiker, always hire a guide as few trails are marked and conditions can be dangerously changeable.

Kasbah du Toubkal; Imlil; tel: 0524 48 56 11; www.kasbahdutoubkal.com; daily B, L, D; map D5

143

Spend the day at a **restaurant with a 360° view**

In the foothills of the Atlas are several enchanting retreats where you can have lunch, lounge by the pool or explore the surrounding countryside.

The village of **Ouirgane** (with a souk on Thursdays) has some of the best places. Rustic **La Bergerie** is set in 12 acres of gardens surrounded by undulating hills. The pool has tempting day beds and the restaurant (by the fire in winter, under a Berber tent in summer) serves both French and Moroccan food. Activities include mountain biking, horse riding and trekking. Lunch at **La Roseraie** – seasonal, organic and locally-sourced – is served either by one of three pools or in the cosy restaurant. There is also a spa and hammam, horse-riding, hiking and watersports on the nearby reservoir.

The pool of **L'Oliveraie**, near Asni, is big enough to be a small lake. There are good lunch menus including use of the pool and transfers back to Marrakech. The **Auberge Au Sanglier qui Fume** is a charming old favourite, with tables under a vine-covered gazebo, delicious French food, a pool, billiards and mountain biking. Prices at all of the above range from 150–300dh for a two course lunch.

All the sites below: map D6
La Bergerie; Ouirgane; tel: 0524 48 57 17; daily L, D
La Roseraie; Ouirgane; tel: 0524 43 91 28; www.laroseraiehotel.com; daily L, D
L'Oliveraie; Route d'Amizmiz, after Asni; tel: 0524 48 42 81; www.oliveraie-de-marigha.com; daily L, D
Auberge Au Sanglier qui Fume; Ouirgane; tel: 0524 48 57 07; www.ausanglierquifume.com; daily L, D

Ski on the highest slopes in Africa and have lunch in a French chalet

There aren't many places in the world where you can say that you have skied in the morning and sunbathed in the afternoon. The ski resort of **Oukaïmeden**, an hour from Marrakech (hire a car or take a grand taxi; map E6), sits at 2,650 metres (8,700ft). The season, if there is snow, runs roughly from late December to the end of March and the pistes range from nursery to a rather hairy black run. There is little in the way of piste grooming so conditions can be rough and as rescue services are virtually non-existent and the nearest hospital is in Marrakech, skiing off-piste is inadvisable.

There are six button lifts and one chair lift – the highest in North Africa, at 3,243 metres – to the top of **Jbel Oukaïmeden**. A viewpoint with an orientation table is set at the top, with sweeping views south to Toubkal and northwards to Marrakech. There are prehistoric rock engravings along the north side of the plateau. Ancient skis and boots can be hired from the bottom of the piste and a donkey will carry you and your equipment back from wherever you end up.

On winter weekends, Oukaïmeden becomes packed

with Moroccans flinging themselves down the slopes on makeshift toboggans and very serious French skiers. The skiing here may not be first class, but a day spent in the sparkling mountain air is a wonderful escape from Marrakech. The real draw is **Chez Juju** (p.140, E6), a rustic French-style chalet restaurant and hotel. Feast on delectable wild boar sausage casseroles with bottles of rich red wine and pay no more than 150dh. You could almost be in the Alps if it weren't for the donkeys...

Be transported to a **country idyll** in the **Ourika Valley**

The Ourika River, which flows down from the High Atlas, is the lifeblood of Marrakech and the verdant **Ourika Valley**. With precariously perched traditional Berber villages that haven't changed in centuries, hillsides abundant with fruit trees and emerald-green terraced fields, it's a delightful country idyll. During summer weekends, the valley is full of picnicking Marrakchis, but this whole area has much that is of interest throughout the year.

The Route d'Ourika, leading out of Marrakech, is lined with garden centres and the odd stall selling fabulous wickerwork furniture and iron lanterns. The Ourika Valley proper starts 30km from Marrakech and the village of **Tnine Ourika** is at its heart. There are several good local restaurants along the main street, where you will also find stalls selling argan oil, fossils, carpets and jewellery.

Just outside town is **Nectarome**, a beautiful garden brimming with scented flowers and herbs. Founded by an aromatherapist, everything here is made into essential oils and natural products, which are sold in the little shop. Call in advance and they will whip up a simple and tasty Moroccan lunch for about 100dh. After, you can indulge in a herbal foot bath whilst gazing out at the mountains. **La Safranière** is a saffron farm, where you can visit the fields, workshops and a little saffron museum to learn about the extraordinary history and culture of the crocus, whose pollen sells like gold dust. The flowering season is in November.

Nearby in the village of **Tafza**, known for its pottery, is the **EcoMusée Berbère**, run by the same owners as the **Maison de la Photographie** (*p.87*) and situated in a traditional pisé building. With the help of the local

people, the museum has been filled with a collection of carpets, jewellery, clothing and pottery. Old photographs are on display and there are documentaries to watch – all illuminating the world of the Berbers. The museum also organizes walks into the countryside, visits to pottery workshops and farms. At the end of the valley, just before the High Atlas really begins, is the **Kasbah Bab Ourika** (map E6), a stunning eco-friendly hotel and dreamy place to have lunch and a swim. Situated on its very own mini mountain, with some of the most spectacular views in Morocco, the Kasbah has a fantastic menu mixing Berber, Arab and international cuisine with the emphasis on fresh, healthy food such as roasted beetroot salad with rocket, feta and walnuts; salmon fish cakes with caper butter and frozen amaretto parfait with medjool dates...

Nectarome; Tnine Ourika; tel: 0524 48 24 47; www.nectarome.com; daily; map E7
La Safranière; Ferme Boutouil Takateret, Km34, Tnine Ourika; tel: 0524 48 44 76; daily 8am-6pm; charge; map E7
EcoMusée Berbère; Tafza, Ourika; tel: 0524 38 57 21; Tue–Sun 9.30am-7pm; charge; map E7

Have lunch by the **seven waterfalls of Setti Fatma**

Beyond the **Ourika Valley** *(p.146)* is the Berber village of **Setti Fatma** (map E6). Once a quiet rural backwater, Setti Fatma's seven waterfalls have transformed it into a bustling hive of tourism, but if you avoid summer weekends, it's still a charming place in gorgeous surroundings.

Clinging to the side of the mountain, surrounded by snowy peaks and dominated by a rosy pink mosque, the village rests at the very edge of a surging river and in the spring, when the waterfalls are at their most torrential, the place is fragrant with almond blossom.

Reaching the first 10 metre (33ft) -high waterfall is an easy 20 minute walk. On longer hikes to reach the other six, you will need a guide (use an official guide from the *bureaux des guides*

on the main street). This more strenuous 2-3 hour walk can be made on foot or with a mule, and little side hikes along the river can be taken. This is the best way to see the countryside in its unspoilt glory, where you will encounter locals tending flocks of sheep, working in their orchards or washing clothes in the river.

Take your own picnic up here or return to Setti Fatma for lunch, where there are dozens of restaurants on rickety platforms above the water, under the almond trees, clinging to the rocks beside the river and on rooftops. You'll be hungry after your explorations, so the piping hot tagines, piles of fresh bread, salads and the obligatory gallons of hot mint tea will be welcome. There is a huge Berber souk here every Monday.

Laze by **Lake Lalla-Takerkoust**, at the foot of the High Atlas

Just 40km (29 miles) from Marrakech, **Lalla-Takerkoust** (map D7) is a lake created by the French in the 1920s to provide thirsty Marrakech with water and electricity. Over 7km (4 miles) long, this glimmering expanse of turquoise takes the breath away. Days here can be as action-packed or as laid-back as you like.

There are two lovely restaurants on the road that curves round to the right. **Le Flouka** has a pool with views across the lake and a good restaurant on the lake edge, serving typical French fare – *côte de boeuf*, steak tartare – as well as Moroccan specialities. They do a reasonable set lunch menu (230dh for a starter and main) and also have a few charming rustic rooms.

Next door, the **Le Relais du Lac** has a tented camp for overnight stays and a beachy outdoor restaurant serving Moroccan food

(expect to pay around 200dh). They also have a range of activities including quad biking, canoeing and donkey polo. The whole area surrounding the lake is perfect for hikes and picnics.

On the other side of the lake is a wonderful local restaurant, **Amaghouss**, with a few rickety tables and chairs on a shaded terrace. Lunch is basic (not more than 100dh): insanely good grilled chicken, a huge salad and a plate of chips. They don't serve alcohol, but you can bring your own. From the little beach below the restaurant you can take pedalos out into the lake free of charge.

Le Flouka; Barrage Lalla-Takerkoust; tel: 0664 49 26 60; daily L, D; map D7
Le Relais du Lac; Barrage Lalla-Takerkoust; tel: 0524 48 49 43; daily L, D; map D7

Escape to the **Agafay Desert** and spend the day in silent contemplation

Not everyone will have the time to venture into the Sahara, two days from Marrakech, but just 45 minutes away is a desert of such beauty you won't need to. The **Agafay Desert** is a breathtaking moonscape, carved by ancient rainwater tracks. On clear days you can almost touch the High Atlas that rear up to the south. The desert, which was first settled by nomads from the Sahara in the 18th century, seems devoid of life at first glance, but in spring it is carpeted with the green shoots of the nomad's pastures and punctuated with oases...

In one of these you will find **La Pause**, where time has come to a standstill. There is no electricity here so you can appreciate the full effect of a desert night sky with no light pollution. Lunch (around 300dh for 3 courses) is

delicious – pizzas with olives and tomatoes, rocket salad from the garden with home-made cold-pressed olive oil, lamb and prune tagine – and is eaten under black Berber tents strewn with carpets, day beds and cushions. There is a deep green swimming pool and majestic Berber horses that can be ridden out into the limitless desert around. There are also camels and quad bikes for exploring and, a little incongruously, crazy golf in the mini Grand Canyon that edges the property (but don't let that put you off). Just a day spent in this serene and very special place is enough to calm even the most hectic mind.

La Pause; Douar Lmih Laroussiene, Commune Agafay; tel: 0661 30 64 94; www.lapause-marrakech.com; daily L, D; map C7

Take to the air in a thrilling **helicopter ride**

Morocco is a vast country that spans over 400,000 square kilometres (154,440 sq miles), with the distances between places of interest often hundreds of kilometres and entailing several days' travel. The country's natural landscapes are some of the most celebrated and diverse in the world, from towering mountain ranges to surf-battered coastline and from desert to arid steppe. For those visiting Marrakech on a short break, it is impossible to see even a fraction of what this country has to offer. If you want to see Morocco from a compellingly different angle, and in the blink of an eye, what could be more thrilling than a helicopter ride?

The Best of Morocco (www.morocco-travel.com) offers bespoke itineraries involving short helicopter rides of an hour to places like **Kasbah Tamadot** (*p.142*) or longer transfers to desert camps in the Sahara. Prices start from £1,700 for an hour in a helicopter seating up to 6 people. **Voyage to Morocco** (www.voyagetomorocco.com) offers several trips ranging from one to five hours and taking in the Atlas, Toubkal region, palm oases as well as transfers to **Essaouria** (*p.154*) and Merzouga in the Sahara.

Sahara Trek (www.saharatrek. com) will chopper you out over the High Atlas and the stunning Drâa Valley to a desert camp in the Sahara for lunch. Journey time: approximately 5 hours. The beautiful **Dar Azawad**, in conjunction with **La Mamounia**, is offering guests a similar service from Marrakech to their exquisite tented camp in the Saharan dunes of the Erg Chigagga. You'll be back in Marrakech in time for dinner.

Speed through palm groves, countryside and desert on a **quad-biking adventure**

If the idea of lounging by a pool or a sedate round of golf fills you with apathy, why not spice up your holiday with something action-packed and adrenalin-fuelled.

With speeds of up to 80 miles an hour and a range of exciting terrains – from sandy desert expanses to winding tracks through palm groves or rough and hilly off-road style pistes – you can be as adventurous as you like and you'll see the Moroccan countryside from a thrillingly different perspective.

As well as being able to rent quads for beach rides in Essaouira (*p.154*) and in the Agafay Desert (*p.150*), there are various companies that offer quad day trips. **DoSomethingDifferent. com** (www.dosomethingdifferent. com) has two tours daily, year round, at 9am and 2/3pm. For two and a half hours, you will zip through palm groves, sandy desert and local villages. The tours are led by an experienced driver and include a stop for mint tea and traditional crêpes with honey, as well as a drop-off back to your hotel. **Dunes & Desert Exploration** (www.dunesdesert. com) has half-day trips that take you across mountains, through wild oases, dry rivers and a rocky desert, with a stop for tea in a Berber village. Departures are twice daily, at 9.30am and 2.30pm. There is also a full-day excursion that includes a traditional picnic cooked 'on location', with departures daily at 9.30am. Dunes & Desert also has multi-day circuit trips for those who want a little bit more. **Rediscover Morocco** (www.rediscover.co.uk) and **Morocco Adventure Tours** (www.moroccoadventuretours. com) both have similar excursions. Prices for all start at around 500dh per person for two hours.

Explore the **highest waterfalls in Morocco**

At 110 metres (361ft), the **Cascades d'Ouzoud** are the highest waterfalls in Morocco, plummeting through three major and several minor drops. During the spring, when the Oued al Abid river runs high, the falls are magnificent; roaring down bright red cliffs into a jade green pool and the canyon far below, which is edged with lime, palm, pomegranate and olive trees.

Nearby are rickety stalls selling jewellery, pottery and souvenirs and some rudimentary cafés serving simple tagines and soft drinks. At the bottom, you get a sense of the full power of the falls with the crash of water and an Evian spray of mist hanging over everything. There are some charming plastic flower-covered wooden barges here that can be hired to paddle about in.

If you want to get away from the touristy throngs around the falls, head to the source (guides can be found in the village), where you can swim in calm pools encircled by exceptional scenery. Unless you decide to take a picnic on this hike, the best place for lunch (also a hotel) is the divinely rustic **Riad Cascades d'Ouzoud**, which has panoramic views over the surrounding countryside from its roof terrace and a traditional Berber menu (120dh), with ingredients sourced from local smallholdings. The riad can organise guided treks to the source of the river, the nearby medieval village of Tanermelt and to the rural souk of Aït Tagla.

The drive to Ouzoud takes around 3 hours.

Riad Cascades d'Ouzoud; Ouzoud; tel: 0662 14 38 04; www.ouzoud.com; map C8

Drive to enchanting **Essaouira** for a **day by the sea**

Essaouira has been inhabited since Phoenician times, when it made the famous Tyrean purple dye used on the robes of Roman senators. In the 15th century the Portuguese established it as a free port for Europeans engaged in trans-Saharan gold, ivory and slave trading. The town itself was built in the 18th century by Alaouite sultan Sidi Mohammed ben Abdallah, who used it as a base for his corsairs.

It first attracted international attention when Orson Welles filmed his *Othello* here and has long been a magnet for artists and travellers. Winston Churchill visited, as did Jimi Hendrix in 1969 and Bob Marley a year later when the town was a countercultural haven for hippies. Today, it hosts the popular Gnaoua Festival of World Music, the 'Moroccan Woodstock' (www.festival-gnaoua. net). Despite all this, Essaouira remains unaffected. The peaceful medina – a Unesco World Heritage Site – is entirely pedestrian, the souks are a joy to explore and the beach is a mecca for surfers, windsurfers and kite surfers

Place Moulay Hassan is lined with cafés and restaurants (**Café France** (map B3) is popular; for Italian cream don't miss **Gelateria**

ESSAOUIRA'S ARTISTS
Essaouira is popular with artists and strolling round town you will see several fantastic art galleries. The **Damgaard Gallery** (Avenue Oqba Ibn Nafi) has been exhibiting works by Essaouira's painters since 1988. **Galerie la Kasbah** (4 rue de Tetouan) is set in an 18th century riad; there is also **Galerie l'Arbre Bleu** (233 rue Chbanat) and dozens of others dotted about town.

Dolce Freddo; map C2). Have a drink on the terrace at **Taros** (tel: 0524 47 64 07; map B3) with sweeping views across the port. In between the square and the port are the **grilled fish stalls** (*grillades de poissons*), a great place for lunch, where freshly caught fish and seafood is grilled in front of you and served with salad.

The main souks are on **Avenue de l'Istiqual** and **Avenue Sidi Mohammed Ben Abdallah** and between Avenue Oqba Ibn Nafi and Place Moulay Hassan you will find an enclave of carpet and kaftan shops. The **ramparts** (*skala*) face the nearby Iles Purpuraires, now the Iles de Mogador, which in the past were used as a quarantine station for pilgrims from Mecca carrying the plague. **Promenade en Mer** (tel: 0524 47 46 18) runs daily boat trips around the islands, offering a close up view for enthusiasts of the islands' abundant bird life.

Along the **Boulevard Mohammed V** are several fish restaurants, the most popular of which is the **Chalet de la Plage** (tel: 0524 47 59 72) where lunch costs around 200dh per person. At the end of the boulevard are lovely laid-back beach cafés – **Ocean Vagabond** (tel: 0524 78 39 34) is the best (mains for 50dh). Surfboards, kites and windsurfs can be rented from **Club Mistral** (www.club-mistral.com) next door. Outside Vagabond, horses, camels and quads can be hired for beach rides. The **Ranch de Diabet** (tel: 0670 57 68 41) also arranges rides on the beach, into the surrounding countryside and to historic sites.

hotels

Fifteen years ago, most of the hotels in Marrakech were uninspiring and nearly all were situated in the new town, Guéliz. Today, there is a mind-blowing assortment of places that cater to every taste and budget. From charming guesthouses to luxury resorts and large international hotels, there is something to suit everyone. But it is the city's romantic, exotic riads in the medina (800 at the last count) that draw the most tourists and are arguably the most atmospheric and memorable places to stay.

Riads are not traditional hotels: they rarely have a minibar, TV or room service and cannot be easily categorised, but they offer an experience that is hard to beat – the opportunity to stay in an authentic Moroccan house centred around a courtyard, with bags of atmosphere and character. Most riads – which range from the super cheap to the fabulously expensive – provide invaluable local advice on the city and will organise day trips and guided tours. Outside Marrakech there is a scattering of tranquil country escapes, and in the Palmeraie are some of the most exclusive boutique hotels.

It is essential to book in advance over the peak seasons of Christmas, New Year and Easter, and it's always worth looking out for deals and packages at other times.

HOTEL PRICES
Price for a standard double room in high season, including breakfast

€€€€ over €350
€€€ €180–350
€€ €70–180
€ under €70

Historic/Traditional

La Mamounia
■ **Southern Medina**
Avenue Bab Jdid; tel: 0524 38 86 00;
www.mamounia.com; map p.56 A6; €€€€
The 'Grand Old Lady of Marrakech',
La Mamounia is the most iconic
hotel in town, where everyone from
Winston Churchill to the Rolling
Stones have stayed. Having recently
undergone a lavish restoration, she
is back and better than ever. All
rooms have a view of the magnificent
gardens and Atlas Mountains. There
are three elegant restaurants – Le
Marocain, L'Italien and Le Français
– as well as the legendary Churchill
Bar, an award-winning wellness spa
and casino.

La Sultana
■ **Southern Medina**
403 Rue de la Kasbah; tel: 0524 38 80 08;
www.lasultanamarrakech.com; map p.56
C5; €€€
In the heart of the 'Golden Triangle'
of the medina, next to the Badi, Bahia
and Royal Palaces, this palace riad
evokes the grandeur of imperial
Marrakech in a historic setting. There
are 28 suites, all with fireplaces,
antique furniture and marble
bathrooms, as well as private living
rooms and hanging gardens. The
courtyard pool shares a wall with the
Saadian Tombs and there is a jacuzzi
on the huge roof terrace, which has
sweeping views of the Atlas.

Les Jardins de la Medina
■ **Southern Medina**
21 Derb Chtouka; tel: 0524 38 18 51; www.
lesjardinsdelamedina.com; map p.57 C3;
€€€–€€€€
This huge riad, once a 19th century
prince's palace in the historic heart
of Marrakech, has been restored and
converted into a luxury hotel with
36 suites set in some of the most

beautiful gardens in the medina. There are countless tranquil spots to relax, a lovely pool surrounded by palm trees, a chic spa with delicious *Sens de Marrakech* products, a fabulous roof terrace with curtained pavilions and even a cookery school.

La Maison Arabe
■ **Northern Medina**
1 Derb Assehbe; tel: 0524 38 70 10; www. lamaisonarabe.com; map p.80 B1; €€€
La Maison Arabe began its life as a famous restaurant in 1946 and has become one of Marrakech's best-known hotels. The owner, Fabrizio Ruspoli, has poured his soul into making this a special place to stay. There are antiques everywhere, lots of cosy places to sit, elegant rooms, two pools (one in a country club outside town), three restaurants and a spa. It is also famous for its cookery school.

Dar Donab
■ **Northern Medina**
53 Rue Dar el Bacha; tel: 0524 44 18 97; www.dardonab.com; map p.80 D1; €€€
Step into Dar Donab and you step back in time. This awe-inspiring grand hotel used to be part of Dar el Bacha (Pasha Glaoui's palace) next door, and exudes history and atmosphere. There are just five suites and all are decorated in luxuriously traditional Moroccan style. Think carved stucco archways, marble floors and painted cedar wood doors. There are several cosy salons and the lovely pool sits in shaded gardens.

Dar Les Cigognes
■ **Southern Medina**
108 Rue de Berrima; tel: 0524 38 27 40; www.lescigognes.com; map p.57 D5; €€€
Opposite the Royal Palace, there was once a wealthy merchant's house... Today, that house has been transformed by architect Charles Boccara into one of the most opulent hotels in town. With carved stucco archways and elegant bedrooms with roaring fires and four-poster beds, you can imagine you're living the life of a Moroccan sultan (or sultana). The hotel arranges excursions, cookery and photography courses and a 'foodie harvest season', involving olive pressing, picnicking and visits to the spice souks.

Hip Havens

as well as a spa, library, movie room and organic garden, staying here is a lesson in relaxation and pleasure.

Tigmi
Environs
Douar Tagadert el Kadi; Km 24, Route d'Amizmiz; tel: 0524 48 40 20; www.tigmi. com; map p.140 D7; €€€

About 15 miles from Marrakech is a special hideaway on the edge of a traditional Berber village. Tigmi is designed to merge with its surroundings and complement the traditional architecture of the region, but it is also quintessentially modern. The gardens are fragrant and lush and the views from its roof terraces stupendous. Winding corridors and walkways create the feel of a little village; there are two pools and also a spa with resident beauty therapist.

Riad al Jazira
Northern Medina
8 Derb Myara; tel: 0524 42 64 63; www.riadaljazira.com; map p.80 B3; €€

In the heart of the northern medina, this luxury guesthouse is made up of three 17th century riads where traditional Moroccan architectural features are combined with fresh modern design. In one courtyard there is an inviting pool, in another a garden and in the third a fountain. There are 15 suites, several stylish lounges, a wellness centre with hammam, massages and aromatherapy treatments and a Berber tent on the roof terrace.

Riad el Fenn
Central Medina
Bab el Ksour; tel: 0524 44 12 10; www. riadelfenn.com; map p.30 D3; €€€

This extraordinary hotel, owned by Richard Branson's sister, is actually four riads knocked into one cool haven of decadent bohemian luxury. There is some serious contemporary art on the walls by Bridget Riley and Antony Gormley among others, and the individually designed suites all have glamorous touches: from leather floors to pink marbled bathtubs. With three pools, including one on the roof, a bar with a mirrored ceiling,

Riad Noir d'Ivoire
🔲 **Northern Medina**
31–33 Derb Jdid, Bab Doukkala; tel: 0524 38 09 75; www.noir-d-ivoire.com; map p.80 D2; €€€–€€€€

The co-owner of Riad Noir d'Ivoire is a designer and her hotel is the height of elegant, understated luxury. This is a mind-blowing yet subtle place: beautiful antiques placed artfully, a white sofa against a carved wooden door, a candlelit lantern in an alcove, soaring columns, jazz on the piano and linen billowing on the roof terrace. There are nine magnificent suites, two courtyards, a pool, library and gym. Winner of the Traveller's Choice Award 2011.

Riad Tarabel
🔲 **Northern Medina**
8, Derb Sraghna; tel: 0524 39 17 06; www.riadtarabel.com; map p.80 D2; €€€

Riad Tarabel is one of the most beautifully restored riads in the medina. With chic grey woodwork, an unusual grassy courtyard shaded by orange trees, elegant rooms (there are just three) decorated with delightful objects from around the world, three

stunning salons, a roof terrace and hammam, this is the ultimate place to get away from it all, whilst still being at the centre of things.

Riad W
🔲 **Central Medina**
41 Derb Boutouil; tel: 0665 36 79 36; www.riadw.com; map p.31 G1; €€

Minutes from Jemaa el Fna is one of the most stylish riads in the medina. Riad W is the height of simplicity with a fashionable and modern feel – stripped-back wooden doors and exposed brickwork, carefully placed antiques and stylish pieces of furniture. The rooms are cosy, there is a little plunge pool in the courtyard and the roof terrace is a lovely place to unwind and have breakfast or lunch.

Heart of the Action

Dar el Souk
Southern Medina
56 Derb Jdid; tel: 0524 39 15 68;
map p.56 C6; €€
Close enough to Jemaa el Fna to
be in the thick of things, but not so
close as to be unbearably hectic, Dar
el Souk (*pictured*) is located just off
the popular shopping street of Rue
Riad Zitoun el Kdim and minutes
from the sights and palaces of the
southern medina. This vibrant riad
is bursting with flowers and has twin
roof terraces covered in cushions
overlooking the whole of Marrakech.
The rooms are individually and
stylishly decorated and have private
outside seating areas.

Dar Attajmil
Central Medina
23 Rue el Ksour; tel: 0524 42 69 66;
www.darattajmil.com; map p.30–31 D3; €€
Just five minutes from the souks and
Jemaa el Fna, Dar Attajmil – a lovely,
cosy riad set around a pretty, leafy
courtyard – has remained faithful to
the original architecture. There are
just four double bedrooms, making
the place feel homely and intimate,
and a small team catering to all
your needs. The chef whips up
delicious Italian-influenced
Moroccan food and there are also
cookery courses, which include a
guided visit to the local food
market.

Les Jardins de la Koutoubia
◾ Central Medina
26 Rue de la Koutoubia; tel: 0524 38 88 00; www.lesjardinsdelakoutoubia.com; map p.30–31 D2; €€€–€€€€

Just steps from both Jemaa el Fna and Guéliz, Les Jardins de la Koutoubia could not be more convenient, especially for those who prefer not to have to negotiate the medina. This is a big hotel (72 suites) but stylishly designed in the style of a grand palace. There is a pool in the courtyard, a piano bar, restaurant and Clarins spa. On the roof is a glamorous plunge pool, good Indian restaurant and a bar open to the stars.

Riad Meriem
◾ Central Medina
97 Derb Cadi; tel: 0524 38 77 31; www.riad meriem.com; map p.31 G3; €€–€€€

Located in the oldest part of the medina, Riad Meriem is on the fringes of the souks but a haven of peace inside. This beautiful boutique hotel has been stylishly decorated by the American designer owner with art, photography and pieces collected from his travels around the world. At night, lit by twinkling lanterns, it could not be more romantic, and the manager is a wealth of insider information on places to go and things to see in Marrakech.

Dar Vedra
◾ Northern Medina
3 Derb Sidi Ahmed ou Moussa; tel: 0524 38 93 70; www.darvedra.com; map p.80 B2; €€–€€€

A faithfully restored 18th century riad edging the main souks, Dar Vedra has seven beautifully-designed bedrooms and one large suite; a sitting room with open fire, a pretty plunge pool outside that is heated in winter and a fabulous roof terrace, covered with plants, day beds and a gazebo for al fresco lunches and dinners. The views across the medina are some of the best.

Riad Magi
◾ Central Medina
79 Derb Moulay Abdelkader, Derb Dabachi; tel: 0524 42 66 88; www. riad-magi.com; map p.31 G3; €€

Just a stone's throw from the souks and Jemaa el Fna is a quiet area at the heart of which is the charming Riad Magi (*pictured*). The pretty courtyard is shaded by orange trees and there is a little tinkling fountain that calms and cools. The six gorgeous rooms are all decorated in different colours – avocado green, cobalt blue; the staff are fantastically helpful and house parties and Moroccan-style weddings can be arranged on request.

Designer Chic

Riad Porte Royale
⬜ **Northern Medina**
84 Derb el Maada, Diour Jdad;
email: riadportroyale@gmail.com;
www.riadporteroyale.com; map p.80 C4;
€€
Lovingly restored by an English
writer, Riad Porte Royale (*pictured*) is
situated in the spiritual heart of the
northern medina, minutes from the
shrine Zaouia Sidi Bel Abbes, and is
a beautifully calm oasis, filled with
antiques and textiles from all over the
world and with a pretty tiled plunge
pool in the courtyard. The riad can be
rented in its entirety for families or
groups of friends.

Riad 72
⬜ **Northern Medina**
72 Derb Arset Aouzal; tel: 0524 38 76 29;
www.riad72.com; map p.80 C1; €€–€€€
In the heart of the prestigious Dar
el Bacha quarter of the medina, this
hip boutique riad evokes all the
splendour of traditional Moroccan
design and architecture, but with
perfectly judged modern twists. The
four suites are super romantic, there
is a bookshop, a spa with hammam, as
well as the services of a yoga teacher
and masseuse. The roof terrace, one
of the highest in the medina, has
exceptional views.

Dar Tchaikana
⬜ **Central Medina**
25 Derb Ferrane, Azbest; tel: 0524 38 51 50;
www.tchaikana.com; map p.31 G4; €€
It's all about attention to detail at this
incredibly stylish riad. Clean white
rooms are punctuated only by one-
off pieces – an antique, a lantern, a
vintage carpet or contemporary piece
of furniture; it's the exact opposite
of heavy oriental design, yet cleverly
inspired by Africa and Morocco. The
staff are welcoming and discreet, and
the food is excellent.

Riad O2
⬜ **Northern Medina**
97 Derb Semmaria, Rue Sidi Ben Slimane;
tel: 0524 37 72 27; www.riado2.com;
map p.80 D3; €€
Between East and West, Orient and
Occident is Riad O2 (*pictured above
right*) – a breath of fresh air in the
midst of the medina. Here, everything

is calm and zen-like. The exquisite spaces are perfectly designed with a mix of contemporary and antique pieces and are adorned simply, with just bright fabrics and light (the place is fabulously lit in bubblegum brights at night) to create atmosphere. Lunch and dinner can be served on request.

Dar Seven
▇ **Northern Medina**
7 Kaa Sour, Derb Ibn Moussa; tel: 0039 347 743 4272; www.darseven.com; map p.80 D4; €€–€€€

Hotels don't get more serenely chic than Dar Seven, which feels more like a private home than a hotel (it is in fact owned by Princess Letizia Ruspoli, who uses it as her holiday home). The whole place is pure luxury. The white walls, creamy linens and polished grey tadelakt floors are perfectly offset with olive trees, vintage wooden doors, black and white photographs and antiques. There are just four stunning rooms, a salon, reading room and beautiful roof terrace.

Villa Makassar
▇ **Southern Medina**
20 Derb Chtouka; tel: 0524 39 19 26; www. villamakassar.com; map p.56 C3; €€€€

Villa Makassar (pictured below) is a riad like no other. A passionate homage to Art Deco, it has been transformed into an extraordinary space that transports you to 1920s Paris or New York. Each of the ten suites has been inspired by the great Art Deco artists (Mondrian, Delaunay, Dunand) and are equipped with every high tech comfort, as well as open fire, sitting room and private balcony. There is a suitably atmospheric bar, art library, boutique shop and spa.

Cheap and Cheerful

Dar Eliane
■ Central Medina
39 Derb Maada Azbest; tel: 0524 37 57 10;
www.dareliane.com; map p.31 G4; €–€€
In the heart of the souks, Dar Eliane
offers all the charm and exoticism of a
Moroccan riad, but without the price tag
so often associated with good quality
places. There is a lovely whitewashed
courtyard, four pretty en suite rooms,
a traditional Moroccan kitchen and
salon with fireplace, and a large roof
terrace complete with Berber tent and
barbecue. Lunch and dinner (all food is
organic) on request and the riad can be
rented in its entirety.

Hotel Sherazade
■ Central Medina
3 Derb Jamaa; tel: 0524 42 93 05; www.
hotelsherazade.com; map p.31 F1; €
Once the house of wealthy merchants,

Hotel Sherazade (*pictured*) is well
located, just south of Jemaa el Fna,
and is excellent value for somewhere
so close to the main square. The riad
is spotlessly clean and run by helpful
multi-lingual staff; most rooms have en
suite bathrooms, those on the terrace
have shared facilities. Day trips to the
Atlas, Ourika Valley and the Atlantic
coast can be arranged on request.

Dar Soukaina
■ Northern Medina
19 Derb el Ferrane, Riad el Arous;
tel: 0661 24 52 38; www.darsoukaina.net;
map p.80 D2; €€
Don't be put off by the scruffy
alleyways you have to negotiate to
get here. This is a blissfully peaceful
little riad decorated with refreshing
subtlety – whitewashed walls, simple
fabrics, gentle colours. Two courtyards

are shaded by a huge orange tree and banana plants and there is a secluded roof terrace with a cushion-filled Berber tent. The nine charming rooms are situated around the courtyards, there is a decorative pool, and dinner can be arranged on request.

Tlaatawa Sitteen
Northern Medina
63 Derb el Ferrane, Riad el Arous; tel: 0524 38 30 26; www.tlaatawa-sitteen.com; map p.80 D3; €

Tlaatawa Sitteen is a great budget option in the heart of the medina, run by charming Moroccans who warmly welcome families into their traditional riad and will help with excursions and tours. It's all about simplicity and homely comforts here. The six rooms are basic but stylish, with shared bathrooms. Delicious and very good value dinner is available on request.

Angel's Riad
Southern Medina
6 Derb Houara; tel: 0524 38 02 52; www.angelriad.com; map p.56 D5; €

Deep in the kasbah of the medina is a very special riad. Owner, Claudia, a Greco-Armenian has brought her love of travel and her passion for colour and light to this exuberant, fun, charmingly bijoux riad. The place is splashed with pink cushions and painted lanterns, blue walls, green tables and a scattering of cherubs here and there. The four rooms are bright jewels and the staff are fantastically helpful.

La Terrasse des Oliviers
Northern Medina
79 Derb Derdouba; tel: 0524 38 72 48; www.terrasse-des-oliviers.com; map p.80 C3; €€

The service could not be more welcoming and cheerful here (pictured), where all is light, bright and happy. The wonderful courtyard is a true riad garden, with trees and plants tumbling everywhere and the roof terrace, shaded by olive trees and bougainvillea, has lots of private corners to relax. All the rooms are comfortable and have lovely personal touches and the chef Malika's home-cooked food is to die for.

Urban Escapes

La Renaissance Hotel
Guéliz
89, Corner of Boulevard Mohammed
Zerktouni & Ave Mohammed V;
tel: 0524 33 77 77; www.renaissance-
hotel-marrakech.com; map p.104 C4;
€€

Established in 1952, Hotel La
Renaissance *(pictured left)* has
long been a landmark hotel in
the buzzing heart of Guéliz. The
hotel is situated in a tall Art Deco
building and recently underwent
a transformative revamp that has
turned it into one of the sleekest,
most contemporary urban hotels
in Marrakech. Guests need only
step outside and they are on the
doorstep of some of the best shops
and restaurants in town. The stylish
rooms are also very good value.

Bab Hotel
Guéliz
Corner of Boulevard el Mansour Eddabi &
Rue Mohammed el Beqal; tel: 0524 43 52
50; www.babhotelmarrakech.com; map
p.104 C3; €€€

For those who would rather avoid
the hustle and labyrinthine alleys of
the medina, the Bab Hotel *(pictured
right)* in the Ville Nouvelle is a die-
hard urban sanctuary and temple to
modernism and minimalism, in the
slick white style of St Martin's Lane
in London. There is no exoticism or
orientalism here – just fresh white
rooms, slate-floored bathrooms
and a hip bar and good restaurant
downstairs that is always lively.

Sofitel
Hivernage

Rue Harroun Errachid; tel: 0524 42
56 00; www.sofitel.com; map p.125 G1;
€€–€€€

Designed in contemporary Arab-
Andalusian style, the Sofitel
Marrakech *(pictured)* is located in
the most prestigious part of Guéliz
and comes with everything you
would expect from an international
five star resort hotel: air-conditioned
rooms with mini bar, TV and Wi-fi; 24
hour room service, three restaurants
serving sumptuous food, three bars, a
nightclub, two huge swimming pools
set in perfectly manicured gardens,
and a spa and fitness centre.

Suite Hotel
Hivernage

Rue Harroun Errachid; tel: 0524 42
45 40; www.suitehotel.com;
map p.125 G1; €€

Although this is in the heart of the
upmarket Hivernage neighbourhood,
the Suite Hotel is excellent value
for money. Each of the 112 rooms
(including reduced mobility rooms)
offers a flexible living space, with TV
and small kitchen. There is a bar, the
'Boutique Gourmand', where you can
buy freshly prepared dishes to eat
in your room; a pool, fitness centre;
business corner with broadband and
the use of a car for stays of 4 nights
or more.

The Lap of Luxury

Amanjena
Environs
Route de Ouarzarzate, Km 12;
tel: 0524 40 35 53; www.amanjena.com;
map p.125 D3; €€€€

Consistently voted one of the best hotels in North Africa and the Middle East, the Amanjena, which means 'peaceful paradise', is the first Aman resort in Africa. There are 32 pavilions bedecked in cedar wood, Venetian glass, marble and rosy *tadelakt*, and six two-storey villas with private courtyards and swimming pools – all set around an ancient irrigation pool at the heart of exquisite gardens of palm and olive trees, with exceptional views of the Atlas mountains in the distance. The hotel is renowned for its trend-setting modern Moroccan design, created by American designer Ed Tuttle, which merges harmoniously with its surroundings,

adopting elements from traditional Moroccan architecture. The spacious grounds encompass a Moroccan/Mediterranean restaurant and a Thai restaurant, a *caidal* tent for special occasions, as well as a spa, library, boutique, a hibiscus-shaded pool and tennis courts. The Amelkis Golf Resort is also just next door.

Royal Mansour
Central Medina
Rue Abou el Abbas Sebti; tel: 0524 80 80 80; www.royalmansour.com; map p.30 A2; €€€€

Built by King Mohammed VI to celebrate the very best in Moroccan design and craftsmanship, this is one of the most spectacular hotels in the world (*pictured*). Accommodation is in one of 53 private riads, each with their own plunge pool. The two restaurants – French and Moroccan

– are supervised by three-starred Michelin chef, Yanick Alléno; the spa has Sisley, Chanel and Dr Hauschka products; the bar has walls of rose gold and the library a star-gazing telescope.

Ksar Char-Bagh
🔲 Palmeraie
Palmeraie, BP 2449; tel: 0524 32 92 44; www.ksarcharbagh.com; map p.125 E5; €€€€

This exquisite hotel, set in 7 hectares (17 acres) of pristine gardens, is arguably more magnificent than most royal palaces. All the 'harim' suites come with a private garden and some with private pool. The French chef concocts fantastic food fresh from the garden and the markets, which can be eaten wherever you like. There is a sumptuous spa, a *fumoir*, a 1,000-book library, a tennis court and even a London black cab to ferry guests around.

Riad Charai
🔲 Northern Medina
54 Diour Jdad; tel: 0524 43 72 11; www.riadcharai.com; map p.80 D4; €€€

Riad Charai was once the residence of the Private Secretary to Glaoui, Pasha of Marrakech. Charai is unique in that there are two buildings at each end of a long garden (rather than around a square courtyard). There is a wonderful pool and the garden, where meals are eaten, is scented with jasmine and orange trees and refreshed by a fountain.

Accommodation is in eight luxurious suites, there's a spa and hammam, and the riad can be rented in its entirety.

Four Seasons
🔲 Environs
1 Boulevard de la Menara; tel: 0524 35 92 00; www.fourseasons.com/marrakech; map p.124 E1; €€€€

Set in 16 hectares (40 acres) of Moorish gardens, the Four Seasons (*pictured*) has arrived in Marrakech and offers everything you would expect. Built as a 'luxury, contemporary medina', there are 141 guest rooms and 27 large suites, all with private balconies and views of the Menara and High Atlas. With a spa, fitness centre, tennis courts, a Provençal restaurant and a brasserie with Moroccan, Italian and Andalusian cuisine, three bars and a kids' club, you could ask for no more.

Les Borjs de la Kasbah
█ **Southern Medina**

Rue du Méchouar; tel: 0524 38 11 01; www.lesborjsdelakasbah.com; map p.57 C3; €€€

This luxury spa hotel *(pictured)* was formed from six small houses and one riad and created by master craftsmen, who have combined luxury mod cons with traditional features. All rooms overlook one of the four original courtyards. The fresh, seasonal menu has been formulated by 2-starred Michelin chef, Olivier Pichot, and fuses French and Moroccan cuisine. The pool and spa occupy their own courtyard and the hotel can arrange excursions and cookery courses.

Baglioni Marrakech
█ **Environs**

Km 8, Route d'Amizmiz; tel: 0524 39 09 30; www.thebaglionimarrakech.com; map p.124 B2; €€€€

Although not scheduled to open until 2013, the Baglioni Marrakech will be one of the most luxurious and exciting new resorts in the world. Set in 14 hectares (34 acres) of breathtaking gardens – designed to feel like a private park, with boulevards, sweeping views and complete privacy – accommodation will consist of 15 four-and-five bedroom residences designed by none other than Jade Jagger. A super swanky spa is also in the plans.

Away from it All

Les Deux Tours
🔲 **Palmeraie**
Douar Abiad, Palmeraie; tel: 0524 32 95 25; www.les-deuxtours.com; map p.124 D5; €€–€€€

Les Deux Tours (*pictured above*) is one of the oldest and most beautiful hotels in the Palmeraie. Built by Tunisian architect, Charles Boccara, it still feels like the private home it once was and is a blissful escape just outside the city. The gardens are lush and dotted with peaceful places to relax, the pool sublime and all the rooms are unique – some even with private plunge pools. Understated and affordable luxury in an impossibly romantic setting.

Le Bled de Grenadine
🔲 **Environs**
KM 5, Route de L'Aeroport; tel: 0661 45 17 90; www.lebleddegre.com; map p.124 B3; €€

This charming country house 10 minutes outside town may not be for everyone , but for those who want delicious home-cooked food, friendly hosts and a relaxed environment in

which to laze about away from the bustle of the city, this is the place for you. Grenadine and Philippe Soubielle have run hotels for years and bring a little French *joie de vivre* to 'Le Bled' and to everything they do. This is also their home and they will make you feel instantly relaxed, going out of their way to help you have as peaceful or as action-filled a holiday as you want. Lunch and dinner – a mix of Moroccan and Provençal – comes from local markets and from Grenadine's garden, which is full of donkeys, dogs, cats, turtles and rabbits. The inviting pool has views to the High Atlas in the distance and is surrounded by day beds and hammocks. The rooms on the first floor have the best views.

La Pause
■ Marrakech Region

Douar Lmih Laroussiene, Commune Agafay; tel: 0661 30 64 94; www.lapause-marrakech.com; map p.140 C7; €€

Forty minutes from Marrakech, in the heart of the Agafay desert, is La Pause (*pictured on previous page; p.150*), a tranquil retreat nestled in its own olive oasis. There is no electricity – everything at night is lit by candles and lanterns. Bedrooms are in Berber tents or simple pisé houses. The pool is shaded and there are tents with day beds for dining. You can go horse or camel riding, or quad biking, all amid the breathtaking desert landscape.

Beldi Country Club
■ Environs

KM6 Route du Barrage; tel: 0524 38 39 50; www.beldicountryclub.com; map p.124 B2; €€€

Set in several hectares of stunning rose gardens that stretch as far as the eye can see, this is a wonderful retreat, just 15 minutes outside Marrakech. Rooms are decorated in rustic style (*pictured*) and set in lush gardens, which are dotted with beautiful pavilions and quiet places to sit. There are two elegant pools, with good restaurants next to each, a spa, and artisanal workshops where you can buy pottery, linens and carpets.

Rose Sultan

Environs
Km 11, Route d'Ourika; tel: 0673 66
71 65; www.rosesultan.com; map p.124
D1; €€€

Just 15 minutes from the centre of
Marrakech is a cool, calm sanctuary.
Rose Sultan is sleekly modern, yet full
of charm. The suites are comfortable
and elegant, the gardens full of roses
and dominated by a huge pool; there
is a roof terrace with spectacular
views and excellent food. It's a bit
like staying at a friend's luxurious
house, with all the benefits of five star
service. The villa can also be rented in
its entirety.

La Ferme Berbère

Environs
Km9, Route de l'Ourika; tel: 0661 22
09 41; www.lafermeberbere.com; map
p.124 D2; €

La Ferme Berbère is a rural retreat
that is a blissful escape, yet within
easy reach of the city. Built using
traditional materials and in the style
of a Berber home, and set in lush
bird-filled gardens, there are cosy,
brightly-coloured salons, shady spots
to sit in the garden, a lovely pool, a
large choice of excursions including
visits to local pottery, jewellery and
carpet ateliers, a traditional hammam
and delicious home-cooked food.

Dar Zemora

Palmeraie
Rue el Aandalib, Palmeraie; tel: 0524 32
82 00; www.darzemora.com; map p.124
D4; €€€

This gorgeous country-style retreat
(*pictured*) set in spacious grounds
in the heart of the Palmeraie is a
wonderful place to get away from it
all. With a pavilion billowing with
silk curtains, scattered cushions and
carpets to laze about in, a delicious
pool and what feels like acres of
grassy rose-filled gardens that flicker
with hundreds of candles at night,
Dar Zemora is also wonderfully
romantic – and intimate: there are
just three bedrooms and three suites,
all with private terraces.

Essentials

A

Admission Charges

Visits to most of Marrakech's monuments and museums are subject to an admission charge. This is normally a small fee of about 10–30dh. If a custodian fulfils an extra service, such as providing a short tour, it is usual to give a tip.

B

Budgeting

Eating Out: A three-course meal for two with Moroccan wine in a mid-range restaurant will cost about 600dh; a coffee about 20dh; and a beer 40–60dh depending on the venue. You can eat in a good but basic grill restaurant for about 150dh for two.

Transport: Hiring a small car for a week costs from around dh3,500. Hiring a *grand taxi* and driver for the day costs around 800dh, depending on distance, often more if organised through your hotel.

C

Childcare

Moroccans are very welcoming of children, including in restaurants; however, that may not be the case in some of the foreign-owned riads, so be sure to check that children are welcome when you book. Nappies and formula milk are widely available, usually in grocery shops rather than pharmacies. Some of the larger hotels offer babysitting services.

Climate

The best times to be in Marrakech are late autumn and early spring. Winter is usually bright and sunny, and sometimes warm enough to swim, but it can also be cold, especially at night when temperatures can drop to below freezing. Mid-summer is usually too hot for comfort as temperatures average 33°C (91°F) and top 40°C (104°F).

Clothing

In summer pack light cottons; in winter be sure to take both light clothes for daytime and warm clothing (including a coat) for the evening.

Also remember that Morocco is an Islamic country so avoid wearing revealing clothing on the streets. In the evenings, smart-casual is acceptable for most venues. You won't get into some of the more exclusive hotels, like La Mamounia, wearing jeans.

Crime

Crime is not especially common, but you should take the usual precautions: use a safe in your hotel; don't carry too much cash on you; keep an eye on bags and valuables; and don't leave belongings visible in a parked car. At night be sure to park your car in a guarded car park.

If you are the victim of crime, you will need to report it to the police (there is a Tourist Police station on the north side of the Jemaa el Fna) and obtain an official report to present to your insurer upon your return.

Needless to say, it is inadvisable to buy or use hashish. There are many Westerners languishing in Moroccan prisons for drug offences.

Customs and Visa Requirements

The airport Duty Free shop is open to incoming as well as departing passengers. Passengers can import 1 litre of alcohol (wine or spirits); 200 cigarettes or 50 cigarillos or 25 cigars; 150ml of perfume or 250ml of toilet water; and gifts up to a value of 2,000dh. You may not import or export dirhams: all local currency must be exchanged in Morocco.

Citizens of the UK, Republic of Ireland, US, Canada, Australia and New Zealand need only a full passport for visits of up to 90 days; the passport must be valid for at least six months after the date you arrive. Visas are not required for stays of less than 90 days. (Visa regulations change, so check before you travel.)

D

Disabled Travellers

Disabled access is generally not good in Morocco. High kerbs in the new town and uneven surfaces in the medina make wheelchair use difficult, and most of the museums occupy old palaces or riads with maze-like layouts and lots of steps. Even when restaurants are accessible, the toilets are rarely so. That said, Moroccans are quick to assist where they can.

Driving

It is not worth hiring a car for getting around Marrakech, as taxis are so cheap, and many places are inaccessible by car; it is worth it, however, if you want to get out and see the surrounding region. However, if you only want to go to Essaouira you are probably better off getting the Supratours bus or the CTM bus, both of which are cheap and efficient.

Car Hire
You can book car hire in advance from home using one of the international companies. However, it is often cheaper to arrange something *in situ*; most companies have offices around Place Abdel Moumen Ben Ali on Avenue Mohammed V. Do try haggling, especially for longer periods. The usual international companies, such as Avis, Hertz and Europcar, all have local offices.

The price for a mid-sized car should be 300dh per day. Four-wheel drives are around 1,000-1,200dh per day.

Rules of the Road
Speed limits are: 40kph (25mph) in urban areas, 100kph (60mph) on the open road, and 120kph (74mph) on motorways (but look out for signs specifying other limits). Be careful to

observe these limits: speed-traps are common, especially on approaches to towns. You will receive a small on-the-spot fine for breaking the speed limit.

The old French system of *priorité à droite* (right of way to traffic coming from the right, i.e. vehicles on a roundabout give way to vehicles coming on to it) is being phased out. However, it is still the case on some roundabouts, so approach with care.

As a rule, Moroccans drive quite chaotically but slowly. Dangerous overtaking on main roads is common, so again be cautious.

Petrol Tips
Petrol stations are plentiful except on routes through the Atlas, where you should be sure to fill up in advance. Forecourt attendants normally fill the tank for you, and may also clean your windscreen and headlamps (a small tip is welcome but not essential).

Breakdown
Your car hire company should provide you with the number of their breakdown company. Otherwise, flag down a fellow driver and ask for a lift to a repair garage in the nearest town to get assistance.

Parking
Your riad or hotel will be able to advise on parking. If they don't have their own car park, you will need to park in a public carpark or on the street. Either way, a *gardien*, who wears an official badge, will keep an eye on your car for a small charge (3–4dh is sufficient for an hour or two, but overnight parking usually costs 15–20dh).

E

Electricity

The electricity supply is rated 220 volts in all but the very oldest hotels. Plugs are the round two-pin continental type, so bring an adaptor if you want to use UK or US appliances.

Embassies/Consulates

Moroccan Embassies
UK: 49 Queen's Gate Gardens, London SW7 5NE; tel: 020-7581 5001 www.moroccanembassylondon.org.uk
US: 1601 21st Street NW, Washington, DC 20009; tel: 202-462 7979; http://dc usa.themoroccanembassy.com.

Moroccan Consulate
US: 10 East 40th Street, Floor 23, New York, NY 10016; tel: 212-758 2625; www.moroccanconsulate.com.

Embassies in Morocco
British Embassy: 28 Avenue SAR Sidi Mohammed Souissi, Rabat; tel: 0537-63 33 33; www.ukinmorocco.fco.gov.uk
US Embassy: 2 Avenue Mohammed el Fassi, Rabat; tel: 0537-76 22 65; http://moroccousembassy.gov.

Emergencies

In an emergency, use the following telephone numbers:

Police: 19
Fire service/ambulance: 15
The tourist police office is on the north side of the Jemaa el Fna.

Etiquette
In the interests of tourism, Marrakchis are fairly tolerant of the behaviour of foreigners, but it is polite to be respectful of Morocco's Muslim culture and avoid wearing revealing clothes in the medina or indulging in overt displays of physical affection (although holding hands is fine). During Ramadan try to avoid eating, drinking and smoking on the streets in daylight hours.

Non-Muslims cannot enter working mosques in Morocco.

F
Festivals
The festival calendar is getting busier year on year, as new festivals are added to boost year-round interest in the city. Some of the main ones are:
January: Marathon des Sables (Desert Marathon; www. saharamarathon.co.uk).
March/April: Riad Art Expo – art festival staged in the city's many riads; www.riadart-expo.com.
June: Essaouira's Gnaoua World Music Festival takes over the town; www.festival-gnaoua.com
July: The Festival National des Arts Populaires de Marrakech takes place at El Badi Palace, celebrating local folklore; www.marrakechfestival.com.

December: International Film Festival – held in early December in the Palais des Congrès, the Théâtre Royal and various smaller venues. A giant screen is erected on the Jemaa el Fna's western side; www. festivalmarrakech.info.

G
Gay Travellers
Homosexuality is, in theory, illegal, and can incur a prison sentence of three months to three years. It is, therefore, important to approach gay encounters with Moroccans with caution; it could be a set-up or there may be an economic motive. That said, Marrakech has long been a centre for expatriate male homosexuality, and many foreign-owned riads offer discreet places to stay.

H
Health
No vaccinations are required for entry into Morocco unless you have come from a yellow fever, cholera or small pox zone.

If you need to see a doctor or dentist during your stay in Morocco, staff in your hotel/riad will be able to help you in finding one.

Insurance
All medical care must be paid for so be sure to take out adequate health insurance before you travel.

Stomach Upsets

These are easily avoided if a few simple precautions are taken: don't eat food that has been left standing or reheated (food stalls should not be a problem as the food is cooked to order), peel fruit, treat salads with circumspection and only drink bottled water. If you are struck down, drink plenty of water, preferably with rehydration salts, and take a diarrhoea remedy (available at pharmacies).

A local remedy for upset stomachs is cactus fruit, also known as Barbary fig, sold from stands on street corners. For a few dirhams the vendor will peel one or two for you while you wait.

Hours and Holidays

Business Hours

Shops in the medina: Sat–Thur 10am–8pm, some also open Fri.
Shops in Guéliz: Mon–Sat 10am–1.30pm and 3.30–7.30pm, closed Sun.
Banks: Winter: Mon–Fri 8.30–11.30am and 2.30–4pm; summer: Mon–Fri 8.30–11.30am and 3–5pm; Ramadan: Mon–Fri 9.30am–3pm.

State Holidays

New Year's Day: 1 Jan
Independence Manifesto Day: 11 Jan
Labour Day: 1 May
Feast of the Throne: 30 July
Reunification Day: 14 Aug
The King's Birthday and People's Revolution Day: 20 Aug
Youth Day: 21 Aug
Anniversary of Green March: 6 Nov
Independence Day: 18 Nov

Muslim Holidays

These are governed by the Hegira lunar calendar and are, therefore, movable. The holidays get earlier by 11 days each year (12 in a leap year). Exact dates depend on the sighting of the new moon.
Mouloud: The Prophet's birthday.
Aid es Seghir (marking the end of Ramadan).
Aid el Kebir (feast of Abraham's sacrifice of a lamb instead of his son).
Muslim New Year

I

Internet

There are numerous internet cafés and some of the *téléboutiques* also offer internet access. The Cyber Parc at the foot of Avenue Mohammed V has internet booths scattered around the park as well as an indoor internet station. Internet access costs around 8–10dh an hour; many of the better hotels offer Wi-fi.

L

Language

Moroccans speak their own dialect of Arabic, but written communication is in classical Arabic. There are also various Berber dialects, and in the Marrakech region it is *chleuh*. Although most Berbers understand Arabic, few Arabs understand Berber.

French is also widely spoken and understood, although fluency is not as widespread as it used to be, partly because children are no longer taught in French in state schools.

Useful Phrases in Arabic
Hello *salaam aleikum*
Welcome *Ahlan wa sahlan*
Good morning *Sbah l-khir*
Good evening *Msa l-khir*
Goodbye *Beslama/masalama*
How are you? *La bes?*
I'm fine *labes*
Please *'Afak*
Thank you *Shukran*
Yes/No *Iyyeh/Lla*
What's your name? *Ashnu smitek?*
My name is... *Smiti...*
Where are you from? *Mnin nta?* (to a man); *mnin nti?* (to a woman)
I'm from England/the US *Ana men inglatirra/amrika*
Do you speak English/French? *Wash kat-kellem l-ingliziya/l-fransawiya?*
I don't understand *Ma f-hemt-sh*
What does this mean? *Ashnu kat'ni hadi?* (for feminine); *Ashnu kay'ni hada?* (for masculine)
Never mind *Ma'alish*
It's forbidden *Mamnu'*
What time is it? *Shal f sa'a?*

Emergencies
I need help *Bghit musa'ada*
Hospital *Sbitar*
Pharmacy *Farmasyan*
Diarrhoea *S-haal*
Police *Bolis*

Getting Around
Where? *Feen?*
Downtown *Wust l-mdina*

Taxi *Taxi*
Grand/shared taxi *Taxi kbir*
Aeroplane *Tiyyara*
Station *Mahatta, la station*
To/From *Al/Men*
Right/Left *Limen/Lsser*

M
Maps
A free and up-to-date map is distributed by the tourist office but its coverage of the souk area is sketchy.

In addition to the maps found in this book, the best available maps are *Insight FlexiMap Marrakech*, published by Apa Publications; *Marrakech & Essaouira* published by Editions Laure Kane; and Michelin map no. 742, which covers the whole of Morocco and features an enlargement of Marrakech.

Media
Publications
There is a range of daily and weekly publications in French and Arabic. The two main publications in French are the pro-Royal *Le Matin* and the more liberal *L'Opinion*. Weeklies include *Le Journal* and the outspoken *TelQuel*. *Le Monde* is also widely available, as are some English newspapers, but the latter will be at least a day old by the time you buy them. For listings of forthcoming events consult the monthly *Tribune de Marrakech*, *Couleurs Marrakech* and *Marrakech Mag*, available in hotel and restaurant foyers and kiosks.

Television

Most hotels provide CNN and BBC World satellite channels. Morocco has two state-run TV channels, 2M and TVM, which are more interesting than they used to be, providing that you can understand French or Arabic, but far from essential viewing. It also operates two privately run satellite channels, Al Maghribiya and Mid 1 Sat.

Money

Moroccan dirhams (dh) cannot be imported or exported, which means that they cannot be obtained in advance of your trip. On departure you can change unspent dirhams back into hard currency in the airport but you must show exchange receipts totalling twice the amount you want to change back, as well as your flight boarding card. You will need cash for shopping in the souks and for some riads.

The dirham is a reasonably stable currency. Recent exchange rates have hovered around 15dh to £1 sterling, 11dh to €1, and 9dh to $1. Rates vary between banks, so shop around.

ATMs

ATMs are the easiest way of obtaining cash, although your bank may charge you a handling fee as well as interest if you are using a credit card (you can often use debit cards bearing the Cirrus logo, but don't rely on this alone). ATMs are plentiful in the Ville Nouvelle and there are a couple of Banque Populaire ATMs at the top of Rue Bab Agnaou, off the Jemaa el

Fna. The daily limit on withdrawals is currently 2,000dh.

Credit Cards

MasterCard and Visa are accepted in most hotels, petrol stations and the more expensive shops and restaurants. Other cards are less widely accepted.

P

Police

Most matters concerning tourists are handled by the tourist police, who have a station on the northern side of the Jemaa el Fna (tel: 0524 38 46 01).

Post

The main post office (PTT) is on Place 16 Novembre in Guéliz. Stamps are available from tobacconists.

R

Religion

Islam

Morocco is a comparatively tolerant Muslim country, but religion is still the biggest influence on society. The five requirements of Islam – affirmation that there is no other god but God and Mohammed is his Prophet; prayer five times a day (you will hear the call to prayer throughout the city); the observance of Ramadan; the giving of alms to the poor; and making the *hadj* (pilgrimage) to Mecca at least once in a lifetime – are central to many Moroccan lives.

Officially, Morocco follows the Sunni (orthodox) branch of Islam. However, there are many thriving Sufi brotherhoods that promote a more mystical approach to God.

Ramadan
The Muslim month of fasting has some disadvantages for travellers. Restaurants and cafés are much quieter during the day (some even close for the month) and some restaurants that normally sell alcohol do not during this time. It is impolite to eat or drink in public during Ramadan.

Christianity
Marrakech has a small Christian community, served by the little Catholic church in Guéliz (*see p.112*).

T
Telephones
Phone booths are plentiful. They are operated with phone cards sold at tobacconists. In addition you will find *téléboutiques* where you can use coins and get change from the attendant.

To make an international call, dial 00 for an international line, followed by the country code (44 for the UK). Remember to drop the initial zero of the UK area code you are dialling.

Mobile Phones
To use your own mobile phone in Morocco you should check costs with your own mobile phone company before leaving home. Alternatively, you can buy a prepaid mobile phone while in Morocco or a SIM card for use in your own phone. These are available from Maroc Telecom, Inwi or Meditel, which have numerous outlets.

Time
Morocco keeps to Greenwich Mean Time all year round.

Tipping
It is usual to tip porters, chambermaids, other hotel staff if they are particularly helpful, and waiting staff. There are no hard-and-fast rules for the amount: 10 percent would be considered generous.

Tourist Information
The main tourist office is on Place Abdel Moumen Ben Ali in Guéliz (tel: 0524 43 61 79). It is open Mon-Fri 8.30am–noon and 2.30–6.30pm, Sat 9am–noon and 3–6pm.

Tours
There are countless local companies offering a wide range of tours, from short guided tours in Marrakech to excursions into the Atlas and southern Morocco. Two reputable companies are: **Ribat Tours** (6 Rue des Vieux Marrakchis, Guéliz; tel: 0524 43 86 93; www.ribatours.com), which specialises in outdoor activities, and **Terres et Voyages** (Immeuble D1, 8 Avenue 11 Janvier, Bab Doukkala; tel: 0524 43 71 53; www.terresetvoyages.com), a reliable mainstream tour operator, that has an English-speaking owner.

Transport

Arrival by Air

Royal Air Maroc operates a daily flight to Marrakech from London Heathrow via Casablanca. Sometimes this involves a long delay in Casablanca while waiting for connecting flights from other countries in Europe.

Royal Air Maroc in the UK: Langham House, 32–33 Gosfield Street, London W1W 6ED; tel: 020-7307 5800; www.royalairmaroc.com.

Royal Air Maroc in Marrakech: 197 Avenue Mohammed V; tel: 0524 42 55 01; www.royalairmaroc.com.

Marrakech is well served by the following budget airlines:

Easyjet (www.easyjet.com), which flies from Gatwick.

Ryanair (www.ryanair.com), which flies from London Luton.

Thomsonfly (www.thomsonfly. com), which flies from Manchester, London Luton and Gatwick.

British Airways (www.ba.com) has started a route from London Heathrow, and British Midland International (www.bmi.com) also flies from Gatwick and Heathrow to Casablanca and Marrakech.

Airport

Upon arrival you will be required to fill out an immigration form before going through passport control. The arrivals hall has the usual facilities, including a bank and cash machine, and car hire firms. There are two terminals (and a third one to open in 2012): Terminal 2 handles all of the budget airlines.

On departure you will also need to fill out an immigration form before passing through passport control. The café in the departure lounge will take euros as well as dirhams.

From the Airport. Marrakech-Menara Airport is situated 6km (4 miles) from the city centre. There is normally a plentiful supply of taxis outside the terminal. The fare into town should be no more than 80–100dh, although you will probably be asked for about 200dh in the first instance so be prepared to bargain. Drivers will accept euros if you do not have dirhams. There is also an irregular bus service (no. 11) to the Jemaa el Fna every 30 minutes or so.

Transport within Marrakech

Taxis. There are two types of taxi in Morocco: *petits taxis* (greeny-beige livery) and *grands taxis* (large cream Mercedes).

Petits taxis take up to three passengers and can be hired on the street. Fares are very cheap, but the meter is often broken so you must negotiate a set price before you get in the car. It is not unusual for people to share *petits taxis*, so don't be surprised if your driver picks up another passenger or two along the way.

Grands taxis take up to six passengers. You can charter a *grand taxi* for the day or for a longer trip (easily arranged through your hotel, or more cheaply by negotiating directly with drivers at the *grands-taxis* stations). In Guéliz the main station is next door to the train station on Avenue Hassan II.

City Buses. There is a good bus service, although buses can get very crowded. One of the most useful buses for tourists is the no. 1 from Place de Foucauld to Place Abdel Moumen Ben Ali. Other useful routes are nos 2 and 10 for the bus station, and nos 3 and 8 for the train station. The flat fare on all buses is 3.5dh. Payment is made upon boarding; drivers will supply change for smaller notes.

Calèches. Horse-drawn carriages congregate outside the larger hotels and at various points around the city, most notably opposite Club Med on Place de Foucauld. Official prices are posted inside the calèche but be sure to check the price with the driver before boarding *(see also p.36)*.

Trains. The entrance to Marrakech's train station is on Avenue Mohammed VI. The station runs direct services to Casablanca, Rabat, Fez, Tangier and Meknès. For information: tel: 090 20 30 40; www.oncf.ma.

Long-Distance Bus/Coach Travel. Supratours (tel: 0524 47 53 17; www.supratourstravel.com) and CTM (tel: 0524 43 44 02; www.ctm.ma) are the most useful companies. The Supratours office is on Avenue Hassan II, next door to the *grands taxis* and railway stations.

V

Visas and Passports

Holders of full British passports or American passports can enter Morocco for a stay of up to three months without a visa, but their passport must be valid for at least six months after the planned departure date.

W

Websites

National Tourist Office (in French): www.tourisme-marocain.com
National Tourist Office (in English): www.visitmorocco.com
Hotel booking and travel tips: www.morocco.com
Good list of riads and restaurant guide: www.hipmarrakech.com
Online travel guide: www.ilovemarrakech.com
Restaurant listings: www.bestrestaurantsmaroc.com
Listings (sites, hotels) for the major cities: www.morocco-holidays-guide.co.uk
Listings (sites, hotels) for the major cities: www.moroccoguide.com.

Women Travellers

Women travellers do occasionally receive a low level of harassment, but this usually remains a mild irritant rather than anything more threatening. Keep hassle to a minimum by behaving coolly but courteously, wearing modest clothing and avoiding eye contact.

Index

Insight Select Guide: Marrakech
Written by: Tatiana Wilde
Edited by: Siân Lezard
Layout by: Ian Spick
Maps: Apa Cartography Department
Picture Manager: Steven Lawrence
Series Editor: Carine Tracanelli

Photography: All pictures APA Ming Tang
Evans except:
Alamy 43, 44, 48, 60, 64, 68, 69, 72, 77, 91, 112,
116, 137, 144, 164, 165T, 169
Bab Hotel 168B
Beldi Spa 98, 128/129, 174
Corbis 90
Dar el Souk 162
Dar Les Cigognes 160
Dar Zemora 175
Les Doux Tours 156/157, 173T
El Saadi 10, 11, 113, 126
Fotolia 95
Four Seasons 131
Istockphoto 65, 89, 92, 94, 109, 117, 130, 136
La Mamounia 70/71, 122, 132, 158
La Pause 150, 173B
Hotel La Rennaissance 168T
Villa Makassar 165B
Maison de la Photographie 87
Marrakech Art Fair 114/115
Minitero del Gusto 21, 41
Musée de l'Art de Vivre
APA Clay Perry 6, 13, 16T, 22, 35, 37, 39, 45,
58, 76, 108, 111, 120, 121, 127, 133, 142/143, 148,
159T, 163, 172
Photolibrary 16B, 19, 42, 65, 85, 145, 149, 153
Riad el Fenn 46, 161B
Riad W 161T
Royal Mansour 52, 170, 171
Hotel Sherazade 166
Terrasse des Oliviers 167
Tips Images 59
Touria Mogador 119
Basemap data: on p.124–5 derived from
OpenStreetMap © OpenStreetMap and
Contributors, CC-BY-SA

First Edition 2012

© 2012 Apa Publications UK Ltd.
Printed in Germany

Distribution:
Distributed in the UK and Ireland by:
Dorling Kindersley Ltd
(a Penguin Group company)
80 Strand, London, WC2R 0RL
email: customerservice@dk.com

Distributed in the United States by:
Ingram Publisher Services
1 Ingram Boulevard, PO Box 3006,
La Vergne, TN 37086-1986
email: customer.service@
ingrampublisherservices.com

Distributed in Australia by:
Universal Publishers
PO Box 307, St Leonards NSW 1590
email: sales@universalpublishers.com.au

Worldwide distribution by:
Apa Publications GmbH & Co.
Verlag KG (Singapore branch)
7030 Ang Mo Kio Avenue 5
08-65 Northstar @ AMK
Singapore 569880; apasin@singnet.com.sg

Contacting the Editors
Please alert us to outdated information
by writing to:
Apa Publications, PO Box 7910, London SE1
1WE, UK; email: insight@apaguide.co.uk